GETTING INTO

Veterinary School

6th Edition

Mario Di Clemente

Getting into Veterinary School
This sixth edition published in 2007 by Trotman and Company Ltd
2 The Green, Richmond, Surrey TW9 1PL

Editorial and Publishing Team
Author Mario Di Clemente
Editorial Mina Patria, Editorial Director; Jo Jacomb, Editorial Manager;
Catherine Travers, Managing Editor; Ian Turner, Production Editor;
Joanna Franaszczuk, Editorial Assistant
Production Ken Ruskin, Head of Manufacturing and Logistics;
James Rudge, Production Artworker
Sales and Marketing Sarah Lidster, Marketing Manager
Advertising Sarah Talbot, Advertising Manager

British Library Cataloguing in Publication Data
A catalogue record for this book is available from the British Library.

ISBN 978 1 84455 140 8

Typeset by Ian Turner.
Printed and bound in Great Britain by Creative Print and Design (Wales).

Contents

Acknowledgements   VI

Introduction   1

1 | What makes a good vet?   5

The farmer's view   6
Prevention   6
Small animals   7
So why do you want to be a vet?   8

2 | Commitment and experience   13

Starting early   13
Getting more experience   14
Making the initial contact   16
What the vet will want   17
Shaping up in the surgery   18
Checklist of experience   18
Variety and staying power   20

3 | The courses   23

The pre-clinical stage   24
The para-clinical stage   25
The clinical or final stage   26
Extramural rotations (EMR)   28
Notes on the courses   28
Financing your course   35

4 I Applying to veterinary school 39

Taking a broad view 40
Practical experience 40
Academic versus practical 41
*Importance of high A level grades
    and supporting motivation* 41
Open days 41
Course entry requirements 42
GCSE grades 43
AS and A levels 43
Other qualifications 44
Admissions tests 45
Studying outside the UK 45
Submitting your application 45
How many applications to make 46
Alternative courses to apply for 47
Transfer from another degree 47
*Deferring entry and taking
    a gap year* 48
A level predictions 49
*Importance of the personal
    statement* 49
Referee's report 52
Other supporting documentation 52
Mature students 53
What to do if you are rejected 54
Retaking A levels 54

5 I The interview 57

Timing 57
The purpose of the interview 57
Preparation 58
Topical and controversial issues 63
Importance of the interview 63
Demeanour 64

6 I Recent and current issues 67

BSE 68
Bird flu 69
Foot-and-mouth disease 71

Intensive farming   73
Tuberculosis and badgers   74
Fox hunting   75
Fall of dairy prices   76
Dangerous Dogs Act   77
Bluetongue disease   78
Animal testing   78

7 | Career paths   83

Working in practice   84
Teaching and research   86
The government   87
Other career paths   88
Summing up   88

8 | Further information   93

Veterinary schools in the UK   93
Other contacts and sources
   of information   95

ACKNOWLEDGEMENTS

I would like to thank everybody who has contributed to the sixth edition of *Getting into Veterinary School*. I am particularly grateful to James Burnett, Catherine Travers, Maya Waterstone and Marianne Di Clemente for their advice, guidance, and practical support. I would also like to thank Emma Godwin for allowing her UCAS personal statement to be included and everyone else who contributed to the previous editions of this book. Particular thanks should go to the staff and students at the UK veterinary schools, and to both UCAS and the RCVS.

Mario Di Clemente
November 2006

Introduction

In 2004–5, 1351 people applied for entry to veterinary school. Of these, 904 were accepted, a success rate of 67%. A further 118 were accepted through Clearing. For potential vets, the most important question is 'What can I do to make sure that I am in that 67% when I apply?' The aim of this book is to give you that information. However, there is no secret formula that will ensure success. The students who are accepted work hard to gain their places. They are motivated and determined, and their desire to work within the field of veterinary science is deep-rooted and genuine. Having said that, even the most promising candidate will not get a place if he or she does not prepare properly.

This book is about getting into veterinary school – it is not about giving up and trying something else. The tone is a balanced mixture of realism and optimism. No one should underestimate the hard road that lies ahead. Getting into one of the seven veterinary schools in the UK (Nottingham became the seventh in 2006) is just the first stage on the route to becoming a qualified veterinary surgeon with all the inevitable hard work and dedication that follows. The key to success lies within each individual.

Academic ability is absolutely necessary. Unless you have clear potential to study science in the sixth form, this book alone cannot help you. Students attracted towards veterinary science should have a natural academic ability in the sciences. A confident prediction of high grades at A level is a great help – but even that will not be enough on its own to get into one of the veterinary schools. Applicants have to show proof of their interest, enthusiasm and commitment. They have to provide evidence that they really do want to become vets.

So, how do you know that this is the career for you and that you are not wasting your own and everyone else's time? A top priority must be to become so well-informed and acquainted with the work of a vet that you know you have made the right choice of career.

And once you know this, what next? What are the factors involved in course choice? Have you considered all of them? What do the courses have in common? What are the factors that influence the admissions tutors to come down in favour of one well-qualified candidate against another? What happens at interview? What about the various career choices open to the newly qualified vet?

Not only that, but what do customers who use the services of veterinary surgeons look for in a 'good' vet? Does this sound like the kind of profession that would suit you? Putting academic skill to one side for a moment, would you feel comfortable dealing with your customers as well as the animals? The first thing you learn in veterinary practice is that all animals bring a owners with them. How would you handle a sceptical dalesman or an elderly lady anxious and watchful as you come into contact with her beloved pet? Animals play a crucial part in the lives of their owners and whether the vet handles this with tact and understanding will be the deciding factor in both their professional and personal development.

Those charged with the responsibility of helping students make important decisions about their future, careers teachers and careers officers in particular, will find this book helpful as will parents anxious to assist their son or daughter. This book may also help to put off those who feel drawn towards animals for mainly sentimental reasons. They may come to realise that they would not cope so well with the owners – who willingly pay the full cost of the vet's services out of their own pocket because their pet means so much to them. No matter how good you are, you've failed unless you can get your message across to the owner so that the animal gets the right treatment.

A feature of this book is the presence of the student view. Those who are now undergraduates on veterinary courses said that they would have appreciated knowing the views of people in their position when they were at school. Often panels made up of students returning to their former schools to give careers advice do not include a veterinary student. This book therefore includes several student profiles, the first of which is included below. Furthermore, it introduces you to the key features of the available veterinary degree courses, guides you through the UCAS application process, with specific reference to veterinary schools, and provides expert advice on preparing for an interview. Topical and controversial issues will be offered up for consideration, any of which could come up at interview, and career options will be outlined. Finally, useful contacts and sources of information will be suggested in order to allow for further assistance and research.

CASE STUDY   **20-year-old Leo comes from London and is now in the second year of his veterinary medicine course at the Royal Veterinary College. He decided to apply to the college having always lived in London and knowing that he might want to live at, or near, home.**

Leo's ambition to be a vet is deep-rooted: 'From about the age of ten, I knew I wanted to work with

animals one day. We had a dog and three cats at home, and I didn't just like playing with them – I also took a very active and real interest in their health and well-being, which I know many of my friends found a bit strange! I also liked visiting farms. Luckily, for a city boy, I had an uncle who owned a farm in Bedfordshire so during my school holidays I would go and spend time there. I remember spending a couple of weeks there one summer and getting as involved as I could in some of the day-to-day farming chores, like milking and feeding. When I was thirteen I got a part-time job at a local kennels and two years later a local vet invited me to spend time observing him at work during my school holidays. I'd written to him three times, so I think he knew I was serious and committed!

'I worked very hard for my GCSEs and A levels. I suppose I was lucky in the sense that I had an ambition driving me on. I was also extremely well aware of the importance of gaining really high grades at every opportunity. I studied Biology, Chemistry and Psychology to full A2 level and got two As and a B. Nothing gave me more pleasure up to that point than arriving at the Royal Veterinary College on my first day and knowing that this was the next step *en route* to achieving my goal of becoming a vet. Two years on, I'm loving it. I'm doing the course I've always wanted to do. I love working with animals and university life is brilliant. Definitely worth all the hard work!'

So now let's get down to basics ... What actually makes a good vet?

1

WHAT MAKES A GOOD VET?

This question is at the heart of the matter because it is a career aim that calls for considerable sacrifice in terms of time and effort. Every veterinary practice has to organise itself so that someone is on call 24 hours a day for 365 days a year. As one farmer commented, 'A vet needs to have a really good sense of humour to be called out at 3am on a cold night to deal with a difficult calving and having to get down in six inches of muck!' It is certainly not a career for someone lacking in confidence, or who holds back and carries an air of uncertainty.

A good vet will be able to diagnose most things, but if they cannot it is their job to know who can. The secret is to know your own limitations. This is particularly important for the newly qualified veterinary surgeon. 'New vets', according to experienced Cheshire farmer David Faulkner, 'must know when to seek help and be mature enough not to be too embarrassed, for there are always a lot of new things still to learn.'

THE FARMER'S VIEW

'Farmers know immediately if they are going to get on with you,' an experienced vet revealed. 'They look at the way you handle and approach the animals. If you can't catch them the owner will lose confidence and you won't be allowed anywhere near the livestock.' A seasoned farmer confided, 'Give me a vet who doesn't wait to be asked and is out giving you a hand.' He added, 'If they are confident in what they are doing it soon comes across.' Farmers and animal owners generally like to have a vet who communicates well, has a sense of humour, is outgoing rather than shy and reserved, and is able to walk into any situation and have an answer.

A recent poll showed that vets are still held in high esteem by the general public. The popular image of a vet is of someone working long hours, who is able and caring, whose charges are not too high and who does not worry too much about bills being paid promptly! People also pictured vets driving around at breakneck speed with a briefcase and a big bag of drugs – the traditional image of an emergency service rushing to reach the scene of a crisis.

PREVENTION

Today there is a lot of knowledge about preventive health by diet and vaccination. Whole herds can be treated at the right time of year. Farmers expect their vet to look ahead and draw their attention to that which will prevent disease: *'Look, October is approaching – why not vaccinate all the cattle and prevent pneumonia?'* Additives can be administered in either the feed or drink. This is much better than having to go through the trauma of having to inject a whole farmyard of pigs! A good vet will seek to promote preventive medicine whenever possible. It makes sense bearing in mind that animals cannot tell you they are not well. A vet can do a lot of good with vaccinations and treating deficiencies through the feed by replacing what is not there, improving not only productivity but also the welfare of the animals.

Most people will agree that prevention is better than cure, but this is not always easy to achieve. Preventive medicine is costly and farmers, in particular, have a reputation for being watchful of how much they spend. There is no doubt that preventive medicine is a good investment for the future but in the aftermath of BSE, foot and mouth, and the collapse of much of their export market, farmers are anxious and unwilling in many cases to make the necessary outlay. Drug usage for cattle has fallen away. Often farmers do not approach the vet until there is an emergency and then you are back to the old emergency service or 'fire brigade' image of the vet rushing here and there.

In today's busy world, with a general shortage of vets, it is not easy to respond to this situation. I heard one experienced vet say that you should still try to take time to stop and let your eyes range over the flock or herd. 'You're not looking at all 300 or so animals, you look for the one or two animals who don't fit into the general pattern and are not looking well.'

A lot can still be done by encouraging good husbandry – by advising on the housing of the animals. A sign of a good vet is that he or she will have the latest drug information at their fingertips and will know how to treat certain conditions. Sound diplomatic advice will also be appreciated: *'Instead of me treating the animals' feet, why don't you improve that footpath?'*

SMALL ANIMALS

With pets, there is great variety – one moment you might be treating a reptile with a nutritional problem; the next, a cat losing weight might be brought in for tests and cause you to wonder if there might be a problem with its liver – or could it be cancer? A rabbit could be brought in – many are now regarded as house pets – and your initial diagnosis of constipation might be confirmed. Dental problems among the small-animal population occur quite frequently but obesity is also much more common than most people imagine. The vet has to counsel the owner on reducing the feed and try to gain acceptance of regular weigh-ins at the surgery.

Most of us live in busy urban environments, increasing the risk of pets being involved in road accidents. A dog that has been hit by a vehicle might be brought in, and the 'crash kit' may have to be brought out. The doses of the most commonly used drugs are marked clearly on the crash box lid, the syringes are loaded, everything is sterilised and ready. It is important to act quickly, but the true professional keeps calm; this is no time for the vet to fumble when decisive action can save the dog's life.

A good vet knows that it is crucial to deal with the owners in a compassionate yet effective way. It has often been said that the hope and trust of the owners is matched only by the trust and helplessness of the animals. To be a good vet you have to acquire that little bit extra. Imagine the scene as a four-year-old becomes distraught when he's told that his pet hamster must be put down. How do you show empathy amid the boy's flood of tears? How do you discuss it with him? Perhaps the boy's parent will let you attempt to explain how the hamster feels and that soon the small animal's pain will cease and the end itself will not be felt. Even when you know it is the kindest thing to do, giving a lethal injection is still one of the toughest parts of the job.

SO WHY DO YOU WANT TO BE A VET?

This is a question worth asking, because it is not a career that will lead to riches or glamour. So why do so many talented students find themselves attracted to the idea of becoming a vet?

Perhaps it is about adapting and fitting into a way of life. Is this what keeps everyone focused during the long hours of study? The interest in and sympathy for animals is taken for granted by many commentators, but in reality it is the way you react to an emergency that puts dedication to the test. A cat is hit by a car, you know that life is slipping away, but you do your best for the distraught owner. You battle to save an animal's life in a freezing barn in the middle of the night. It is all in the vet's day or night's work and there is no one to applaud you except the grateful, or not so understanding, owner. In short, commitment is the key, particularly if, or perhaps that should be when, the going gets tough. As a vet you must feel that you want to help, cure and take care of animals to the best of your ability whatever the weather and whatever the circumstances. It is the kind of commitment which will almost certainly have begun at a very early age and will have become stronger and more focused with your passing teenage and college years. Of course, not all qualified vets are in general practice. Whilst the vast majority are, other career options are also open to you such as teaching, inspection or research. Yet no matter which option you pursue, the level of knowledge and commitment required is very high.

But back to general practice (where most of you surely hope to end up) and a few words from that most famous of vets, James Herriot, on what it really entails to join the profession and why absolute commitment is essential. In his first book, *If Only They Could Talk*, he reflects that animals are unpredictable things and that a vet's whole life is unpredictable. 'It's a long tale of little triumphs and disasters,' writes Herriot, 'and you've got to really like it to stick it ... One thing, you never get bored.'

Later, on another occasion, Herriot muses, with aching ribs and bruises all over his legs, that being a vet is, in fact, a strange way to earn a living:

> But then I might have been in an office with the windows tight shut against the petrol fumes and the traffic noise, the desk light shining on the columns of figures, my bowler hat hanging on the wall. Lazily I opened my eyes again and watched a cloud shadow riding over the face of the green hill across the valley. No, no ... I wasn't complaining.

Some people grumble about the beguiling influence of the Herriot books. There is, however, a lot of cool reality in the pages laden with good humour and philosophy; so much so that one student described the effect of the books as leaving a 'cold afterglow'. Many professions would love to have a PR agent writing on their behalf with the skills of Herriot.

CASE STUDY Richard sat his A levels last year, and is in his first year studying veterinary science in Scotland. Richard was brought up in London, but his family moved to Essex at the start of his final year of GCSEs. Richard had wanted to be a vet since the age of eleven, when his school went on a visit to London Zoo and were allowed behind the scenes and given a talk by a vet who worked there. 'We had always had pets at home, including cats, dogs and various small animals and birds. At times, home was like an animal sanctuary as my mother was always looking after neighbours' pets. To be honest, I found them all a bit boring, and it was only the visit to the zoo that made me sit up and realise that being a vet involved more than putting down sick animals or vaccinating them when they were young.'

The change of school disrupted Richard's studies. Having been on target for A and A* grades at his previous school, he only managed to gain two A grades. 'Under the old A level system I would have been in trouble because I would have been judged only on my GCSE grades and A level predictions, but mine was the first year to sit AS levels, and I was determined to do well as I knew that if I did, I could show that my GCSE grades were not a true reflection of my ability. I took Biology, Chemistry, Maths and Psychology and got A grades in each one. I then carried on with Biology, Chemistry and Maths and got AAA. I had two interviews, and got an offer from the first one. I was probably overconfident in the second interview, since I already knew I had an offer, and I was surprised to be rejected. Luckily, I got the grades that I needed and so didn't need an insurance offer.'

Richard started getting work experience in the summer following his GCSE examinations. He worked for three weeks on a local farm 'mainly painting fences, but also being able to feed the cattle and help with milking', and spent a further week on another farm near Edinburgh where his uncle lived. 'That is why I decided that I wanted to study in Scotland – not only because I liked the area, but also I thought that I would have an advantage over other applicants since I had worked there.' The following summer, Richard spent two weeks with a vet in a nearby town, mainly concentrating on domestic pets, and a further week with the vet who visited the farm in Scotland. 'I was lucky – my school helped me to organise the first placement with a vet, and my cousin was already shadowing the Scottish vet and she asked him if I could come along. The irony was that I got a place and she didn't! Luckily, she now has an offer for next year but at a different veterinary school.'

Richard has enjoyed the first year of his studies, but finds some of the work hard. 'The pace is different from A level, and it is not just a question of learning notes – they want to find out if we understand as well: not like school! Another thing that makes it harder is that my parents are not around to tell me to do my homework every night, and there are lots of opportunities to go out and enjoy life. Still, I think I am just about coping but I know that I'll have to work harder next term.'

2

COMMITMENT AND EXPERIENCE

Wanting to become a veterinary surgeon is a long-term commitment. It requires perseverance and a lot of determination. If all goes well and you get the kind of sixth-form science results demanded by all the veterinary schools, it will still take a further five or six years to qualify. Most people faced with the need for intensive study in the sixth form will find it hard to look further ahead than the next test or practical. Yet much more than this is needed if you are to stand a chance of getting into veterinary school.

STARTING EARLY

Ideally the pursuit of your interest in animals and their welfare, in short your commitment, should have started much earlier. There are numerous cases of aspiring vets who have begun their enquiries as early as the age of 12, and certainly many have started gaining their practical experience by the age of 14.

Some vets have grown up on a farm and knew that they wanted this kind of life. Others have come from an urban background and have developed an interest despite not being brought up in an animal-friendly, environment. This interest can be started in a variety of ways and can develop through, for instance, pet ownership, the Herriot books, one of the numerous TV programmes like *Animal Park*, *SuperVets* or *Vet Safari*, or the influence of a friend. 'It's a great life, there's so much variety,' was one student's view. 'You realise it when you start going out getting experience. You see that you can be a vet in a town or in the countryside, that some practices are much larger than others and that some are very busy while others appear more relaxed.'

One young vet said that she had begun her enquiries at about the age of 14 and started working at weekends – her experience began with work in a stables where she began to learn horse riding. Another recalled how she had done kennel work at weekends for four years before becoming a veterinary student. It goes without saying that cleaning out kennels is a dirty, often unpleasant job, but to do this over such a long period shows an impressive degree of commitment and dedication from an early age. Some students have the chance to gain early experience on a nearby farm. But what would you do there? One farmer's wife commented, 'We would expect a 14-year-old to help feed the livestock, to help with bedding-up, which means putting fresh straw in the pens and sweeping up.' You should be alert to what is happening around you. Before long you may start asking questions: 'Why is that calf coughing? What are you giving it?'

GETTING MORE EXPERIENCE

As those pre-A level years unfold it makes sound sense to follow up the visits to the local stables, kennels or farm with a week or two with your local vet. The point is that you are not just trying to find ways to satisfy an admissions tutor at veterinary school who may one day read an application that you have completed, important though that is; you are also testing your own motivation. This is vital, for make no mistake, you are going to need all the focus you can muster. The task you are about to set yourself is going to draw upon all your commitment, dedication and determination.

It should be pointed out that a student who is still at school or sixth-form college will be very lucky to find themselves in the consulting room with the vet. This is because anxious owners will not always appreciate or understand the need for someone of school age to be present. It is much more likely that you will be asked to spend time with the veterinary nurses. As one vet commented, 'Let's see if they can handle animals. Are they frightened?' The idea is to see how the student reacts to aspects of animal husbandry at an early stage. If you cannot abide cleaning up the blood and faeces that goes with animal practice then you should in all probability seek out another career and save yourself and others a lot of wasted time. After an artery has stopped pumping or diarrhoea has ended, there is a clean-up job to be done and that is an early experience for many well-intentioned potential vets. Can you take it?

Confirmation of a period spent at a veterinary establishment is one of the conditions for entry to an undergraduate course leading to the degree of Bachelor of Veterinary Medicine or Science. Without getting out and finding what it is like to deal with sick animals as well as normal, healthy ones, how will you know that you are suited to a career dedicated to providing a service to animals and their owners? As one student put it, 'Knowing what animals look like doesn't necessarily prepare you for what they feel or smell like. There is only one way to find out and that is to get into close contact.' You may think you love animals because of the way you feel about your own pet, but going from the particular to the general may cause you to think quite differently. So check it out, you might even be allergic to some animals. Make certain that you still feel happy about dealing with animals in general and really mean business.

Work experience is also vital if you are to have a chance of being called for interview, and without an interview you cannot be offered a place. Some of the veterinary schools are more specific than others about what they expect in the way of practical experience. The Royal Veterinary College, for example, specifies 'at least six weeks "hands on" experience: two weeks with one or more veterinary practices; two weeks or more working with larger domestic animals on a livestock farm; and two weeks of other animal experience (eg kennels, riding school, zoo etc)'. Cambridge is more relaxed about work experience. The Cambridge website states that 'it is helpful to have some personal experience of the veterinary profession and have a realistic idea what the work may entail. However, extensive experience is not a prerequisite and seeing a variety of different aspects of the profession for relatively short periods can be more helpful.' Glasgow advises applicants that 'experience working with veterinarians, so that the applicant has some understanding of the duties and responsibilities of a practitioner, is essential before making such a career choice.'

MAKING THE INITIAL CONTACT

Making the initial contact can also be quite difficult, often because of your nervous inexperience or because the vet is cautious and reluctant to take on an unknown commitment. This is where parents can help, particularly when you are pre-sixth form. If a parent knows that their son or daughter is serious and is showing promise at school in the sciences, they can be a real help by speaking to the vet and giving reassurance. Generally vets will react favourably to a parent's call because it means that the contact is serious. Once the initial opening has been made the ensuing development of contacts is best left to you as part of your growing self-reliance.

Your local vet will know a lot of people through working with animals. A recommendation, or better still an introduction of yourself by your local vet to a large animal practice or a local farmer, may lead to work in a stables or work with sheep, for example. You will get to know people yourself and this builds your confidence. Developing contacts in this way is known as *networking*.

Taking the initiative like this can do you more favours than always relying on the careers department at your school. However, it is worth checking to see whether your school careers department can help you. Frankly, some school careers departments are much better organised than others. If the careers programme is well organised and planned on an established contact basis it would be sensible to enlist the department's help. However, do bear in mind that there is concern among some vets that placements organised by schools are not always carefully matched. If you have any doubts on this score, you will be well advised to take the initiative in making your own arrangements. Remember that in the end it is your own responsibility to get practical experience. Busy people like vets and farmers are likely to be more impressed with those who exhibit the confidence and self-reliance to make their own approaches.

WHAT THE VET WILL WANT

Some vets express reluctance to allow young inexperienced people into their practice. This is understandable. They know that many people are attracted by the idea of becoming a vet; they have, after all, seen many TV programmes! Look at it from the vet's point of view. Some people are attracted to animals for emotional reasons; some may not be academically strong enough to make the grade; some may be so impractical that they could get their finger nipped through one of the animal cages in the first half hour. Do not be surprised if some vets suggest that you should first visit for just a day. The reason for this is that they feel they need to meet you first before committing themselves. As one vet said, 'You can get a fair idea in the first few hours; some are bright and a pleasure to have around.'

What will the local vet ask you to do? This will depend upon the vet. 'We cannot afford to waste time so we begin by asking about their capability for science A levels at grades A and B,' remarked one vet. 'We give them three days of blood and gore to see what it is all about. In our case, they will see a farm. We insist on wellies and a good standard of dress, no jeans or open-necked shirts!' Alternatively, your local vet may be a small practice dealing mainly with companion animals – most often cats and dogs, but also rabbits, goldfish, gerbils and budgies. Some students may themselves have gained experience breeding bantams, ferrets, pigeons or fish. This all points to a strong interest.

Some practices are mixed, dealing with farm animals, horses and pets, while in country areas there are practices that deal mainly with farm animals. The type of practice and its size varies widely. The average practice has three or four vets, while at the one extreme about 2% have more than 10, each with a degree of specialisation; at the other end of the scale, about 25% are single-handed practices, requiring practitioners to deal with a wide range of work. This being so, the resources that the vet will be able to draw upon will also vary widely.

SHAPING UP IN THE SURGERY

A head nurse in a medium-sized mixed practice uses the following six headings to enable her to judge how students helping in the small-animal surgery are shaping up. They are all well worth considering.

- How keen are they to help in every area? For example do they clean up willingly?
- How observant are they? Do they watch how we do the bandaging or how we hold the animal straight ready for an injection? Do they watch carefully how we take a blood sample, administer an anaesthetic or set up an intravenous drip?
- Do they maintain a neat and tidy appearance and clean themselves up before going in to see a small-animal client? This is very important to the owner.
- Are they friendly towards the client? Do they make conversation and try to establish a relationship?
- Do they ask questions about what they do not understand? They shouldn't be afraid to ask even while procedures are being carried out.
- Are they listening to what is being said and the way it is being said? Do they appreciate the experience that allows the vet to counsel owners on sensitive issues? For example, on reducing their favourite pet's diet. This is not an easy message to get across to an over-indulgent owner and it needs a good bedside manner for the vet to be able to tell the owner what must be done without giving offence.

CHECKLIST OF EXPERIENCE

Always take up any opportunities that you are offered. Variety of experience will not only broaden your understanding of the profession you seek to join, but will also impress the admissions tutors when they come to scrutinise your UCAS application. Here are some suggestions. Remember, some applicants to veterinary school will have carried out some of these suggestions four or five years before applying! Others are only applicable to Year 11 or sixth-form students. But if you can tick every box by the time you submit your online form in October of your upper-sixth year, well done!

- ☐ Get work experience in catteries and/or boarding kennels.
- ☐ Work in the local pet shop.
- ☐ Make contact with a local vet and indicate your interest by helping with some of the menial tasks. If you are keen you will not mind the dirty work.
- ☐ Get at least two to three weeks' experience with a large-animal veterinary practice or occasional days or weekends over a long period. Without this, you will not be taken into veterinary school no matter how well qualified you are academically. You must also gain some experience of working in a companion animal practice. Some candidates are fortunate in having access to mixed practices in which they can gain familiarity with handling large and small animals.
- ☐ Visit a local dairy farm and get acquainted with farmwork, which accounts for at least 30% of all veterinary science work. Try also to assist on a sheep farm at lambing time.
- ☐ Organise experience working with horses at a riding stables. (Remember that riding establishments are subject to inspection by an authorised veterinary surgeon.)
- ☐ Arrange to visit an abattoir if possible.
- ☐ Get in touch with one of the animal charities, such as the People's Dispensary for Sick Animals (PDSA) or the Royal Society for the Prevention of Cruelty to Animals (RSPCA), and find out about their work.
- ☐ Do not ignore the chance to spend a day in a pharmaceutical laboratory concerned with the drugs used by vets as well as medics or a laboratory of the Department for Environment, Food and Rural Affairs (Defra).

☐ Try for any additional relevant experience that may be within your reach, eg at a zoo, where you could work as an assistant to a keeper, or in a safari or wildlife park.

☐ Make a point of visiting local racecourses and greyhound tracks, paying particular attention to how the animals are treated. Maybe your local vet has a part-time appointment to treat the horses or dogs. If the offer comes to visit with the vet you should take it.

☐ Visit country events like point-to-point races, even if it is only to see what goes on. One day you may get an admissions interview and the more you know about what happens to animals in different situations the better.

VARIETY AND STAYING POWER

It is crucially important to demonstrate variety in your practical experience with animals. A visit of just one day to a different veterinary practice where you watched small animal work, followed by another visit to a mixed practice where you were able to see a surgical procedure carried out will be impressive, particularly if you can combine this with stables work, some contact with local farms and at least some experience in, for instance, a set of kennels.

But your application to veterinary school will be enhanced even further if, in addition to this, you can demonstrate a convincing commitment to one or two of the local professionals. What will impress people is the fact that you have willingly returned to your local vet's practice over a period of time and only the vet will know what it has cost you to do this. True, you have seen a lot of interesting and varied activities and met many interesting people, but the truth is that many of your friends would have melted away had they been asked and expected to do what you have had to do. Let's face it, not many students would have returned to the practice after having to clean up and deal with blood and muck time and again.

If you can demonstrate both a variety of experience and a committed staying power, there is no doubt that this will count strongly in your favour when the competition for places in veterinary school is at its fiercest.

CASE STUDY   Sarah studied for her A levels at an independent
school in London. Her interest in veterinary
science started when she was allowed to spend a
day with a vet at a small private zoo when she was
14. In the first year of A levels, Sarah tried to organise work experience, but found it difficult since she
was an accomplished sportswoman and musician,
and so she had school commitments on Saturdays,
as well as most evenings. The veterinary practices
and animal welfare organisations that she contacted
wanted volunteers to work on a regular basis, and
she was unable to do so. Realising the need for
work experience, Sarah looked for other opportunities.

'I managed to arrange to help out in a Riding for
the Disabled centre, on Sundays, where I cleaned
the stables and fed the horses. Although this was
hard work, it meant that I could have contact with
a local vet, who visited the stables every so often.
Through him, I was able to spend a week with a
friend of his, who had a practice in Dorset, and this
led to my being able to spend a month on a dairy
farm in the summer holidays.

'I had never regarded myself as being what you
might call pushy, but I found that if I demonstrated
my enthusiasm, and asked for help with a smile on
my face, people were only too glad to help me. I
realised that I had to try to use contacts that I had
made to gain work experience if I was to succeed in
convincing the veterinary schools that I was
serious. Of course, the point of my work experience
was not only to persuade the selectors but, more
importantly, to prove to myself that I really wanted
to be a vet.'

Sarah sat A levels in Chemistry, Biology and
Mathematics, gained AAA, and is now studying
veterinary science in Scotland.

3

THE COURSES

Given the competitive nature of entry into veterinary school, the idea that there is an element of choice may seem strange. Even when a candidate is fortunate enough to get two or three offers, and has to express a preference, the eventual decision is often based upon things like family connections, the recommendation of the local vet or whether or not the candidate liked the school or its locality on the open day.

Maybe decisions should be made upon more objective data than this, but they seldom are. This may not be a bad thing as decisions made this way often work out quite well. However, although the courses are not vastly different, it is surely sensible for the candidate to be aware of the typical course structure and what is involved. This could be useful at interview. Most importantly, a knowledge of some of the differences between courses could play a part in your decision should you get two or more offers.

All the courses leading to a degree in veterinary science have to comply with the requirements of the Royal

College of Veterinary Surgeons for recognition under the Veterinary Surgeons Act 1966. This is necessary if the degree is to gain for the holder admission to the Register which confers the legal right to practise veterinary surgery. It follows that the courses are fundamentally similar; most of the slight differences come towards the clinical end of the degree. This is quite a contrast to many other degrees where the differences can be much more marked.

Veterinary courses have a carefully structured and integrated programme with one stage leading logically into the next. This logic is not always apparent to the student who may feel surprised at the amount of theoretical work in the early pre-clinical stage. Later, as you get into the para-clinical and clinical stages, it all begins to make sense. As one final year student commented, 'It's not until the fourth or fifth year that you suddenly realise "So that's why we did that!"'

THE PRE-CLINICAL STAGE

The first two years are pre-clinical and include not only a lot of lectures, but also practicals and tutorials. The normal healthy animal is studied. A basic knowledge of the structure and function of the animal body is essential to an understanding of both health and disease. The scientific foundations are being laid with an integrated study of anatomy and physiology. This study of veterinary biological science is augmented by biochemistry, genetics and animal breeding, as well as some aspects of animal husbandry.

VETERINARY ANATOMY

This deals with the structure of the bodies of animals. It includes: the anatomy of locomotion; cellular structure; the development of the body from egg to newborn animal; the study of body tissues such as muscle and bone; and the study of whole organs and systems such as the respiratory and digestive systems. Studying this subject involves anatomical examination of live animals with due emphasis on functional and clinical anatomy. Students spend a lot of their time examining the macroscopic and microscopic structures of the body and its tissue components. One student said, 'We seemed to look through microscopes for hours at various organs and tissues. At the time it was not easy to see the relevance, but later what we had been doing began to make a lot of sense.' There is not only detailed microscopic study of histological sections but also the study of electron micrographs of the cells which make up the different tissues.

VETERINARY PHYSIOLOGY AND BIOCHEMISTRY

This examines how the organs of an animal's body work and their relationship to each other. This is an integral part of the first two years of the course. It is concerned with how the body's control systems work, eg temperature regulation, body fluids, and the nervous and cardiovascular systems. You can expect that your studies will include respiration, energy metabolism, renal and alimentary physiology, endocrinology and reproduction.

ANIMAL HUSBANDRY

This extends throughout most courses and introduces the student to various farm livestock and related aspects of animal industries. The kind of performance expected from the different species and their respective reproductive capacities is investigated. Nutrition and housing of livestock are studied, together with breeding and management. Students learn about the husbandry of domestic animals and some exotic species. Animal husbandry also involves techniques of animal handling. These are important skills for the future veterinary surgeon since the patients will often be less cooperative than those met by their medical counterparts. They may even be much more aggressive than humans!

THE PARA-CLINICAL STAGE

This is sometimes referred to as the second stage. This follows on from the first two years in which normal, healthy animals have been studied. Now it is time to undertake studies of disease, the various hereditary and environmental factors responsible, and its treatment. The third year usually sees the study of veterinary pathology introduced (although it sometimes begins in the second year) with parasitology and pharmacology.

VETERINARY PATHOLOGY

This is the scientific study of the causes and nature of various disease processes. This subject is concerned with understanding the structural and functional changes that occur in cells, tissues and organs when there is disease present.

VETERINARY PARASITOLOGY AND MICROBIOLOGY

This deals with the multicellular organisms, small and large, which cause diseases and with bacteria, fungi and viruses. All the basic aspects of parasites of veterinary importance are studied. Students also take courses in applied immunology (the body's natural defences).

VETERINARY PHARMACOLOGY

This is the study of the changes produced in animals by drugs (artificial defences against disease). It comprises several different disciplines including pharmacodynamics (the study of the mechanism of the action of drugs and how they affect the body); pharmacokinetics (absorption, distribution, metabolism and excretion of drugs) and therapeutics (the use of drugs in the prevention and treatment of disease). Some schools introduce this subject in the fourth year.

THE CLINICAL OR FINAL STAGE

The last two years build on the earlier years, with food hygiene being introduced while the study of pharmacology is deepened. The meaning of the phrase 'integrated course' now becomes apparent as all the disciplines come together. Medicine, surgery and the diseases of reproduction are taught by clinical specialists in the final stages of the course, which is largely practical. More time is spent at the school's veterinary field station. In some cases you can expect to live in at the field station in your final year. Much of the study will be in small groups. In some cases you will be allowed to pursue particular interests. However, the main focus will be on diagnosis and treatment by medical or surgical means necessary for the prevention, diagnosis and treatment of disease and injury in a wide range of species.

SOME PRACTICAL SKILLS USED IN THE CLINICAL STAGE

There are many important practical skills that students have to learn in the final clinical period. One of these is to be able to examine the contents of the abdomen through the wall of the rectum without harming the animal or infecting themselves.

You can also learn to use an ultrasound probe to examine, for example, the ovaries. Another use of ultrasound is to listen to the foetal heart sounds of a pregnant sow and the blood flow. Ultrasound can also assist in carrying out an examination of a horse's fetlock.

Students, like the vets they hope to become, can be called out in the middle of the night to a difficult calving. If a cow cannot give birth naturally, the student can help with a caesarian operation. Using a local anaesthetic allows the operation to take place with the cow standing, which makes the process easier to manage. Practical skill is important with foaling. It is best if this takes place quickly because it is less stressful for the foal. Students are taught that all that is needed is a gentle but firm pull. Final-year students can assist with the lambing, even the birth of twin lambs.

There are many examples too numerous to mention. The use of general anaesthetic can extend from a full range of horse treatments to vasectomising a ram. Many other techniques are taught. Students can, for example, look at images of the nasal passages of a horse and see the nasal discharge from a guttural pouch infection. Another example is learning the right way to trim a cow's foot. All animals (that have them!) can suffer problems with their legs or feet.

The experienced veterinary surgeon has to have the skill and confidence to be able to remove a cyst from a sheep's brain without causing a rupture. No wonder then that it is at this final clinical stage that the student finds that all the earlier preparation comes together and makes sense as clinical problem after problem requires you to think and reason from basic scientific principles.

Examples like these do convey the varied nature of the veterinary surgeon's work, but it is as well to remember that in addition to the physician side of the job there is a lot of routine 'dirty' work. Students have, for example, to help maintain cleanliness in the stables and enclosures of the field station. In due course, when you become a working vet, you may at some stage spend time, on a cold wet day, tramping round a muddy farmyard carrying out blood testing of hundreds of cattle.

Beware though that this brief summary of some of the clinical work encountered on the courses is far from comprehensive and should not lead students to believe that this corresponds to a job description.

EXTRAMURAL ROTATIONS (EMR)

This is sometimes called *seeing practice* and the time is divided between farming work and experience in veterinary practice. Students are required during the first two years to complete 10–12 weeks of livestock husbandry, depending on which school you attend. The students usually arrange this experience themselves to take place during their vacations, and on the whole they do not seem to have too much difficulty.

Veterinary schools have lists of contacts that can be made in their own area. A modest amount of pay can be arranged between student and farmer. During the third, fourth and final clinical years students must complete approximately 26 weeks of seeing practice. This will be mainly with veterinary surgeons in mixed general practice, with much shorter periods in, for example, laboratory diagnostic procedures and one or two weeks in an abattoir. Casebooks have to be kept and presented at the final examination.

NOTES ON THE COURSES

BRISTOL

An interesting feature of the course at the University of Bristol is that students are taught by pre-clinical departments who also teach science, medical and dental students. It is suggested that this encourages cross-fertilisation of ideas and access to the latest research findings in other scientific fields. **Assessment:** This is by examination, normally in January and June each year. **Resits:** There is a chance to resit all or part of the examination in September if the required standard is not reached in June. **Intercalation:** It is possible to interrupt your studies for a year at the end of the second or third year in order to gain additional training for a BSc degree in, for example, Biochemistry, Microbiology, Pathology, Pharmacology or Zoology. **Clinical training:** The Clinical Veterinary School is at Langford in the Mendip Hills, about 13 miles out of Bristol. Appropriate extramural experience abroad is allowed at Bristol. There is a Veterinary Laboratories Agency nearby.

CAMBRIDGE

This is the smallest of the veterinary schools. The course extends for six years and is divided equally between the pre-clinical and clinical parts. The first two years are concerned with the basic medical and veterinary sciences, between which there is much common ground at this early stage, bringing you into contact with students from other disciplines. There are also more applied courses in farm animal husbandry and preparing for the veterinary profession. For the third year you can elect to study in depth a subject of your own choice from a wide range of options, leading to the award of the BA (Hons) degree at the end of Year 3. The flexibility of the tripos system is one of its most attractive features. **Clinical training:** The clinical training course is taught in the Department of Veterinary Medicine at the West Cambridge Campus on Madingley Road. The emphasis is on small-group practical teaching. The final year is largely lecture free with hands-on experience and a period of elective study. The Farm Animal Practice provides first-opinion clinical services to surrounding farms including the University Dairy Farm just a few miles away. A new Farm Animal Referral Centre was opened in 2002. Advantage is also taken of the nearby RSPCA clinic, specialist equine practices in and around Newmarket and the Animal Health Trust Centre. New facilities for equine work and a new Small Animal Surgical Suite have just been completed. A thriving research environment ensures that veterinary teaching is embedded in the latest cutting-edge discoveries.

EDINBURGH

Long established and one of the larger veterinary schools, the Royal (Dick) School of Veterinary Studies can trace its origins back to 1823. The school is now part of the College of Medicine and Veterinary Medicine. Traditional boundaries between subjects have been reduced. Most of the pre-clinical training is at Summerhall, close to the city centre. Formal teaching is completed in four years, with the final year devoted to clinical experience. **Assessment:** Half of the assessment is continuous, with the balance by examination and practicals. **Resits:** There is a chance to resit the examinations in August if the required standard is not met in June. **Intercalation:** It is possible for students to interrupt their studies at the end of Years 2,3 or 5 to take a BSc (VetSc) degree in Biochemistry, Neuroscience, Microbiology and Infection or Pre-clinical Sciences. Also available is a one-year MSc by research after the third year of studies and the possibility of doing an intercalated three-year PhD during the course of studies. **Clinical training:** This takes place at the Easter Bush Veterinary Centre, six miles south of the city. This houses the college farm which is attached to the University's School of Agriculture, the Large Animal Practice, Equine and Food Animal Hospitals and the new Small Animal Hospital. The Centre for Tropical Veterinary Medicine forms part of the school. The BBSRC's Moredun Research Institute, the Roslin Institute and a veterinary investigation centre are situated nearby.

GLASGOW

This is one of the larger schools, founded in 1862. The school has the unique advantage of being situated on a single site at Garscube, four miles to the north west of Glasgow. Some pre-clinical teaching is held at the main university campus near to the city centre, which enables students to benefit from the opportunities at both sites. **Resits:** These can take place in September of each year. A second failure may result in repeating a year; normally this is only possible for one year of the course. **Intercalation:** It is possible at the end of Year 3 to study for a one-year BSc (VetSc) Honours before starting the clinical training. Eight subjects are available. A two-year intercalated BSc Honours degree at the end of either Years 2 or 3 is another possibility. **Clinical training:** Glasgow was the first school to introduce the lecture-free final year. This was done in order to maximise the opportunities for small-group clinical teaching around live animal cases. This takes place at the Faculty's busy referral hospital and through extramural study undertaken in practices and other veterinary institutions in the UK and overseas.

LIVERPOOL

The university was the first to establish a veterinary degree. The Faculty of Veterinary Science celebrated its centenary in 2004. There are two degree courses leading to BVSc MRCVS – the D100, which is a five-year course, and the D101, which is six years incorporating an intercalated BSc. The options for intercalating include a BSc in Conservation Medicine and an MSc in Veterinary Infectious Disease and Control. These courses are also offered to students from other veterinary schools. In 2001 the Faculty also introduced a three-year Honours BSc course in Bioveterinary Science. Teaching on this course is shared between the Faculty of Veterinary Science and the School of Biological Sciences. Veterinary students spend the first three years of the course on campus in Liverpool studying pre-clinical and para-clinical subjects. The course is modularised. During the fourth and final years, the students are based at Leahurst, the teaching hospital on the Wirral Peninsula 12 miles away. This has excellent facilities for equine and livestock cases. The Small Animal Hospital is currently sited in Liverpool. A new-referral Small Animal Hospital is being built at Leahurst, and is due for completion in 2007, although first-opinion work will continue at Liverpool. There are two separate practices operating out of Leahurst, serving the large local equine population and the agricultural sector. Farm visits and investigations extend to the sheep farming areas of North Wales and the dairy farms of Cheshire and Lancashire. Horses suffering from conditions such as colic, skin tumour and orthopaedic conditions are referred from all areas of northern England. Leahurst is in

close proximity to Chester Zoo and there is a strong
interest in wildlife diseases and animal behaviour.

LONDON

The Royal Veterinary College, based in Camden Town, is
the oldest and largest of the seven UK veterinary schools.
The college aims to provide an enlightened, innovative
and scientifically based veterinary undergraduate curriculum. Students spend their first two years undertaking
comprehensive pre-clinical studies at the Camden
campus, and then proceed to clinical studies at the
Hawkshead campus in Hertfordshire (north of London).
Resits: These are held in September. It may be possible to
retake a year if necessary. **Intercalation:** It is possible to
intercalate a BSc after successful completion of, normally,
the second year. Students are able to attend BSc courses
offered by University of London colleges, at other universities, or the RVC's own Veterinary Pathology course.
Clinical training: The final year is lecture-free and
devoted to intramural and extramural rotations through
the College's veterinary hospitals and private veterinary
practices. During the course 38 weeks of extramural
study must be carried out. It is possible for some of this
to be undertaken overseas. The substantial elective period
allows in-depth study and the opportunity to complete a
clinical research project.

All of the courses aim to produce a graduate with sufficient breadth and depth of knowledge that he or she will
be able to adapt to the changing demands of the profession over the 40 years or so of working life.

NOTTINGHAM

Based at the university's Sutton Bonington Campus,
Nottingham's School of Veterinary Medicine and Science
accepted its first students in 2006. It aims to provide a
progressive, dynamic environment and to equip students
with all the necessary diagnostic, medical and surgical
skills. Its course integrates clinical medicine and surgery
with pathology and basic sciences, thereby ensuring that
its graduates gain the best possible foundations for a

career in the veterinary profession. Studies will include time spent at the new purpose-built clinical teaching facilities and at local clinical practitioners. The five-year degree course leads students from day one through a clinically integrated curriculum providing learning in all aspects of veterinary medicine and surgery. In Years 1 and 2, students undertake a minimum of 12 weeks animal husbandry extramural studies and at least four weeks of clinical EMS in Year 2. In Year 3 all students undertake a research project and in both Years 3 and 4 a minimum of 12 weeks of clinical EMS is undertaken. The summer term of Year 4 and the whole final year is spent in clinical rotations. This will include a minimum of 10 weeks EMS. A further 25 weeks of Intramural Rotations (IMR) are undertaken in Year 5. IMR may include time at both large and small animal practices, laboratory facilities and specialist facilities. After five years of successful study the degrees of Bachelor of Veterinary Medicine and Bachelor of Veterinary Surgery are awarded.

TABLE 1: STUDENT NUMBERS 2005*

		First year admissions		Second year admissions (or later)		Admissions with a degree		Total no on course		No taking intercalated course		No holding intercalated degree		No graduating (2005)	
		Male	Female	Male	Female	Male	Female	Male	Female	Male	Female	Male	Female	Male	Female
Bristol	UK	24	90	0	3	0	18	137	382	1	9	12	20	36	45
	EU	0	0	0	0	0	0	0	1	0	0	0	0	0	0
	Other	2	0	0	0	0	0	4	5	0	0	0	0	2	1
Cambridge	UK	18	49	0	0	1	4	105	283	0	0	0	0	16	45
	EU	0	1	0	0	0	0	0	3	0	0	0	0	0	0
	Other	0	1	0	0	0	0	0	1	0	0	0	0	0	0
Edinburgh	UK	18	73	3	7	4	17	101	370	0	4	9	16	20	61
	EU	1	2	1	1	2	2	9	9	0	0	0	0	1	0
	Other	3	15	0	7	0	7	7	51	0	0	0	0	0	8
Glasgow	UK	27	51	1	4	2	2	124	297	2	2	3	0	19	67
	EU	0	0	0	0	0	0	1	0	0	0	0	0	1	1
	Other	15	24	0	2	10	22	36	72	0	0	0	0	1	5
Liverpool	UK	19	82	3	15	6	20	136	387	5	10	7	18	28	55
	EU	0	1	0	1	0	1	1	2	0	0	0	0	0	3
	Other	0	0	0	0	0	0	4	6	0	0	0	0	3	4
London	UK	31	174	4	17	4	18	143	764	7	26	16	47	22	96
	EU	0	2	0	1	0	1	1	12	0	2	0	0	0	1
	Other	4	12	0	0	3	12	15	59	0	1	0	1	6	19
Nottingham	UK	19	69	–	–	5	17	–	–	–	–	–	–	–	–
	EU	1	4	–	–	0	0	–	–	–	–	–	–	–	–
	Other	0	1	–	–	0	0	–	–	–	–	–	–	–	–
Total		182	582	12	58	37	141	824	2704	15	54	47	102	155	411

* Sources: Royal College of Veterinary Surgeons Annual Report 2006; Nottingham Veterinary School (figures for 2006)

**FINANCING
YOUR COURSE**

Once you arrive in veterinary school you will want at least to avoid the worry of getting too deeply into debt. It is, of course, true that money is a problem for all students and not least with vets who have additional expenses connected with their course. These extra costs can be summarised as being mainly travel expenses, clothing, books and equipment. Veterinary students are also limited in the opportunities they have to earn extra money during vacations due to the extramural rotations spent gaining prescribed experience in veterinary practice as part of their training. Students believe that sixth-formers and others approaching veterinary school should be forewarned and prepared to cope with the money side of being a veterinary student.

First-year expenditure for veterinary students is particularly high and can easily exceed £8000 for those living away from home.

TABLE 2: EXPENDITURE ESTIMATE PER PRE-CLINICAL YEAR

	London	Away	Home
Tuition fees*	£3000	£3000	£3000
Overalls	£55	£40	£40
Lab coats	£50	£35	£35
Wellies	£35	£35	£35
Course notes	£75	£75	£75
Textbooks	£300	£300	£300
Travel costs	£420	£365	£365
EMS travel costs	£310	£290	£290
Student vet sub	£60	£60	£60
Social events	£1200	£1200	£950
Accommodation	£4000	£3500	n/a
Total*	**£9505**	**£8900**	**£5150**

*Scottish and non-UK EU students studying in Scotland pay £1300 less in tuition fees.
Please note: These figures were estimated in November 2006 and are intended only as a guide.

HINTS AND TIPS

■ Avoid buying lots of kit or textbooks in advance. When you get to the course you may find some discounts available. Second-hand textbooks may be for sale, although many veterinary students prefer to keep their textbooks for use in their working lives. Try medical students as well for second-hand textbooks.

■ Check for student travel concessions, get advice on the best offer on the regular trips that you will have to make.

■ It is a good idea to apply for the student loan early on as it takes some time for the loan to be processed. You can also make contact with the bank about that overdraft facility they promoted to you when they sought your custom.

■ Veterinary students work hard and like to play hard as well. Set yourself a limit on how much you are prepared to spend each term. Remember – the more partying, the worse your bank account will look. Perhaps you will go to the annual vet ball. If you do, why not consider buying the gear second hand? By all means join the Association of Veterinary Students (AVS), but do you want to attend the congress or go on sports weekends? They all cost money.

■ Easter is a time when it is possible for students to augment their income. Once you have gained experience with your first lambing, students say that it is possible, if you are lucky, to make over £300 per week. This is very hard work involving 12 hours a day, for seven days a week, for a minimum of three weeks. But it will certainly improve the look of your bank account – and give valuable experience.

CASE STUDY   Daniel is in the fourth year of his veterinary studies. He has opted to follow a six-year course which incorporates an intercalated BSc degree. His third year involved research projects in other departments of the university, and he gained a BSc in Anatomy. The reason that Daniel chose the intercalated BSc course is that his interests lie in the field of veterinary research rather than practice. He has a particular interest in equine medicine and behaviour and chose his university because of its strong links with an equine hospital.

Daniel gained nine A grades at GCSE, and chose to study Biology, Chemistry, Physics and Psychology at A level. 'My interest was always in the theoretical side of my science A levels – I used to hate practical work at school. I was always breaking things and my experiments would never work. It became a joke amongst my teachers and the others in my classes. When I told them that I wanted to study veterinary science at university, it caused great hilarity. My careers teacher gave me lots of help in preparing for my interviews, and we decided that the best option was to be very honest about my interest in research rather than try to pretend that I wanted to be a practising vet. Most of my work experience was in research. My school helped me to arrange some placements at Birmingham University during my A levels, working with post-graduates on molecular biology, and I was able to bring along reports to my interviews. I managed to get four A grades at A level, but it was a close run thing because I didn't get high marks in my Biology and Chemistry coursework, and my Physics practical exam was a disaster. The veterinary course is very practically focused and I have discovered that I enjoy this more than I thought I would. Not enough to make me want to change direction, though! My aim is to work in a university research department, and possibly in a pharmaceutical company later on.'

Most of Daniel's friends on the veterinary course want to work as veterinary surgeons. They particularly enjoy the practical side of the course, but can sometimes find the theoretical aspects difficult because they seem less relevant to the realities of working as a practising vet. 'Despite the different directions that we want to take in our careers', says Daniel, 'we have one thing in common – we are all absolutely focused on our goals, and we work incredibly hard in order to achieve these. Studying veterinary science is demanding – I am sometimes jealous of friends studying arts subjects at the university because they have so much free time. They also have more money than I do because they all have part-time jobs – something I don't have time to do. However, they do not have clear ideas about where their lives are heading, which I do. I wouldn't swap places with them.'

APPLYING TO VETERINARY SCHOOL

Admissions tutors try to get the best students they can for their course. That is putting it at its most basic. But there is more to it than that. They are also acting in the best interests of the veterinary profession. They know that the competition is fierce and that the biggest hurdle faced by aspiring students is entry into a veterinary school. Once this obstacle is overcome there is, given the undoubted ability of those able enough to get the entry grades needed, every chance that with diligence and lots of hard work the student will in due course enter the profession.

However, it is important to understand that motivation is the key factor in selection. It is, in the last analysis, more important even than A levels or their equivalent. Therefore, the admissions tutors are looking at the total impression conveyed by the candidate on the UCAS application. This will include not only academic predictions and head teacher's report but also extracurricular interests as well as the extremely important supporting practical experience and references. In the final analysis, the tutors know that they are exercising a big responsibility. Their decisions will largely shape the future profession.

TAKING A BROAD VIEW

Ideally, admissions tutors will seek to have students representing a good cross-section of the community. In recent years more women are applying and being admitted than men. Then there is the question of background. Those with an upbringing in country areas can have an excellent range of experience and general knowledge of animal husbandry. Some of them may be the sons or daughters of farmers or vets. Clearly they have a lot to offer. Yet it would be unfair and divisive to fill a course with people who all had these advantages. What of the students coming from the cities where gaining practical experience is not so easy? A few places will be kept for graduates taking veterinary science as a second degree. There will also be some places reserved for overseas students who provide valuable income as well as added richness to the mix of students in all the veterinary schools. Nevertheless, the overwhelming majority of places on these courses will be filled by school-leavers or those who have taken a year out since leaving school.

PRACTICAL EXPERIENCE

Each of the veterinary schools' admissions tutors will seek well-rounded evidence of practical experience and interest. For example, the Royal Veterinary College states that course applicants are expected to have at least six weeks of practical experience made up as follows: a minimum of two weeks with one or more veterinary practices; two weeks' experience of handling larger animals by working with farm livestock; and two weeks of other experience, eg kennels. Another example is Liverpool where they want to see experience with at least three of the six main animal groups – horses, cattle, sheep, pigs, poultry and small animals. An absolute minimum of three weeks of work shadowing with vets is regarded as essential. Note that the phrases 'at least' and 'minimum' occur frequently. In other words, serious applicants should aim to do more to give themselves a chance.

ACADEMIC VERSUS PRACTICAL

Despite the strong emphasis on practical experience demanded by all the veterinary schools, many people in the veterinary profession are concerned that the high A level grades required, currently ranging between AAA and AAB, suggest that the profession is being filled with people who, while being academically very bright, are not so hot dealing with the practical side of the work. Apart from the fact that it is often wrong to assume that academically able people are always very impractical, this worry reveals an imperfect understanding of the logistics of the UCAS (Universities and Colleges Admissions Service) operation each year and how the admissions tutors in the veterinary schools deal with it. Crucial to understanding what happens is the completion by the student of the UCAS application and the evidence of the supporting motivation.

IMPORTANCE OF HIGH A LEVEL GRADES AND SUPPORTING MOTIVATION

Professor Gaskell, when he was Dean of Liverpool's Veterinary School, left no room for doubt that the most important thing from the admissions' point of view is understanding what the prospective student is about and his/her motivation. This has to come across in the student's UCAS application. But that is not to say academic ability is unimportant. There is an enormous amount that has to be learned, and Professor Gaskell advises, 'It's the same with medicine – we find that A levels or their equivalent are good indicators of the ability to absorb, hold and recall information.'

The problem with weaker A levels is that you may start to find the amount of learning required difficult. Fortunately veterinary science is in the position of being able to select the best of the motivated. It must be added that it is not in the interests of the profession, or the animals and their owners whom the vets serve, to relax this strong position.

OPEN DAYS

It is desirable to visit the veterinary schools that hold special interest for you on their open day. Such a visit will give you the chance to see some of the work of the veterinary school. There will be special exhibits, possibly a video programme and most probably the chance to hear the views of the admissions tutor. There may also be the opportunity to visit the veterinary school's own field station where most of the clinical work is done in the final stages of the course, and although veterinary students are kept very busy you may get the chance to speak with some of them. Some schools actually arrange for a number of their students to accompany parties of visitors on the open day. The open day will also give you an opportunity to see the general attractions of each university as a place to live and study over the next five (or six) years.

Your school will receive details of open days with forms to be completed by those wishing to attend. If you have not heard by about a month ahead of the college open day you wish to attend, make enquiries in your school's careers department. If you hear nothing you should take the initiative yourself and write to the school liaison office or directly to the address of the institution which interests you. (These addresses are listed in Chapter 8.) You owe it to yourself to find out as much as you can. Your visit and how you felt about it could also be a talking point should you be called for interview. So do not squander the opportunity to fit one or two visits into your A level study schedule.

If you are taking time out gaining practical experience and have already met the academic requirements, you may be able to get away to attend more open days. If this is the case you may get more than one unconditional offer and so you should certainly try to visit as many of these events as you can.

It is a good idea to make notes after each visit to an open day of your impressions and what differences you spotted. These notes will be very useful if you are called for interview when they will almost certainly ask you about your visit.

COURSE ENTRY REQUIREMENTS

The academic requirements of the seven veterinary schools are similar, but there are differences, and it is important that you obtain the most up-to-date information before deciding where to apply.

Information can be found:

■ In the university prospectuses
■ On the university websites (more likely to be up to date)
■ In *Degree Course Offers* by Brian Heap
■ From the university admissions staff.

Details of all of these can be found at the end of this book.

For A level students, the selectors will take into account:

■ GCSE grades
■ AS choices and grades
■ A level (A2) choices and predictions/grades
■ Any documented extenuating circumstances that might have affected your performance.

GCSE GRADES

You will be asked for 'good grades at GCSE'. What does this mean? It means lots of A and A* grades, particularly in the sciences, English and Mathematics. If you did not get good GCSE grades, you can still apply for veterinary science, but your referee should make it clear why you did not achieve the grades that you needed – there may have been circumstances, such as illness, that affected your performance.

AS AND A LEVELS

Every university student has to meet the general matriculation requirements of each university (consult the prospectuses) but in addition there is the special prescribed subject requirement. You should check the requirements carefully – the veterinary schools' websites carry the most up-to-date information – but it is likely that you will need three A levels (that is, three subjects carried to A2 level), which will include Chemistry, Biology and one other science/mathematical subject. Your choice of AS and A level subjects is vital because, whilst one veterinary school might require three sciences (including Chemistry) at AS level with two taken on to A2 level, others require Biology and Chemistry at A2, or even three sciences at A2. If you are applying to Cambridge, you should be aware that different colleges have different requirements. Currently no veterinary school makes a conditional offer on three A levels at below AAB grades. Unlike the requirements for many other courses, offers are likely to be made on the basis of A level grades only: stand-alone AS levels are unlikely to be taken into account. However, clearly the AS grades are important because they will be stated on the UCAS application, and thus will give the admissions tutors an indication that you are on course for AAA or AAB at A level. For example, when faced with two candidates whose academic backgrounds are identical except that one has AAAA at AS level whilst the other has CCCC, who do you think they would favour?

Some students have been known to query whether they should take a fifth AS level or a fourth A level (not including General Studies). Before doing so you should bear in mind that if you offer four A levels your performance in all four subjects will be taken into account. So if you do feel inclined to add a fourth subject at A level remember the high grades needed for admission.

OTHER QUALI- FICATIONS

For applicants with **Scottish qualifications**, it is likely that you will be asked for AAABB or higher in your Higher grades (SCE/SQA) and Advanced Higher grades in Chemistry and at least one other science subject. Some veterinary schools like candidates to take a new subject at Higher level if only two Advanced Higher grade subjects are taken in the sixth year. Higher grades alone are unlikely to be sufficient.

The **Irish Leaving Certificate** is unlikely to be accepted as equivalent to GCE A level. This is because studying a wider range of subjects to a lower or less specific level than the UK's A levels does not meet the need of the veterinary science course requirements. Therefore, this qualification must be offered in combination with UK qualifications.

The **International Baccalaureate** is usually acceptable provided that appropriate combinations of subjects are studied. Three subjects are needed at the Higher Level. They must include Chemistry and Biology, together with

**ADMISSIONS
TESTS**

ideally one or both of Physics and Mathematics. Grade scores needed in the Highers are likely to be 7, 7 and 6. If the combination is likely to be different, advice should be sought. Similar subject combinations are required by those offering the **European Baccalaureate**. Applicants are likely to need an average score of 8.0, including Chemistry and Biology.

**STUDYING
OUTSIDE
THE UK**

Applicants to certain medicine, veterinary medicine and related courses are required to take the BioMedical Admissions Test (BMAT). The BMAT is owned and administered by Cambridge Assessment, one of the world's largest assessment agencies. Of the seven UK veterinary schools, the test is currently required by Bristol, Cambridge and the Royal Veterinary College in London.

It is possible to practise as a vet in the UK having studied overseas. The process is simpler for students who have studied in the EU, or in certain universities in Canada, Australia, South Africa or New Zealand. However, graduates from other countries can still practise in the UK if they sit and pass the Statutory Examination for Membership of the RCVS, which is held in a UK veterinary school in May/June each year. Further information for all overseas graduates can be obtained from the RCVS website.

An option open to students who wish to study overseas, but want to undertake some of their clinical training in one of the UK veterinary schools, is the veterinary science course offered by St George's University in Grenada, West Indies. Contact details for the course can be found in Chapter 8.

**SUBMITTING
YOUR
APPLICATION**

Applications for admission to veterinary science degree courses have to be made through UCAS. Applications for veterinary science must be received by UCAS by 15 October for entry in the following year. Applications received after this may be considered by the veterinary schools, but they are not bound to do so, and given the number of applications that they will receive, it is likely that they will not do so. In order to ensure that your application reaches UCAS by the deadline, you should complete it at least two weeks before this date so that your referee has time to write his/her report. The current UCAS application should be available via your school or college. However, if you have left school, or have any difficulties accessing the electronic application system, you should write after 1 July in the year preceding entry, to UCAS, Rosehill, New Barn Lane, Cheltenham, Gloucestershire GL52 3LZ.

If you wish to apply to the University of Cambridge, the blue Preliminary Application Form (PAF) can be received by the college of your choice from June onwards and must be received in Cambridge by mid-October at the latest. More information on applications to Cambridge can be found in another book in this series, *Getting into Oxford and Cambridge*. Your completed UCAS application must also be submitted by the closing date of mid-October.

TABLE 3: APPLICATIONS TO UNDERGRADUATE COURSES IN VETERINARY SCIENCE FOR ENTRY IN 2005

	All applicants	Degree accepts	Clearing accepts
Men	294	183	31
Women	1057	721	87
Total	**1351**	**904**	**118**

HOW MANY APPLICATIONS TO MAKE

You may only apply to four Veterinary Science courses. If you apply to more than four, your UCAS application will be returned, and by the time you amend it, you may well have missed the 15 October deadline. A common question is: 'Should I put two non-Veterinary Science choices in the remaining slots?' There are arguments for and against doing so, and you will need to discuss this with your careers advisor or referee. It would probably not be a good idea to apply to Veterinary Nursing, for example, but applying to Equine Science might be. The admissions staff at all of the veterinary schools emphasise that candidates will not be disadvantaged if they fill the remaining places with other courses. However, you should be wary of putting down courses that you are not interested in, and accepting an offer as your insurance place, since you will not be eligible for Clearing if you do so.

Therefore, holding 'insurance' offers will depend on how committed you are to veterinary science. An argument in favour of going all out for the total commitment of applying solely to veterinary schools is that if you fall short of the required grades, and have just missed out, you will almost certainly have the option of gaining entry into an alternative course through Clearing. This is because other pure and applied science courses are inevitably much less competitive and you will be able to accept an offer if you want to do so, although it is more likely to be at a lower-ranked institution.

ALTERNATIVE COURSES TO APPLY FOR

This is a very personal matter but something can be said on what should be avoided. You should not put down medicine or dentistry. Although veterinary science admissions tutors would not automatically exclude anyone because of this mixture, they would certainly look long and hard for overwhelming evidence that veterinary science was what you really wanted. In such circumstances you could hardly expect also to satisfy the medical admissions tutors!

All things being equal it seems logical for applications listing clearly related subjects like agriculture, equine studies, animal physiology, biochemistry, microbiology or zoology to possess that important quality of coherence and to fit in with the general thrust of your application.

TRANSFER FROM ANOTHER DEGREE

If you really want to become a veterinary surgeon, and with hard work you can attain the necessary academic standard, it is not a good idea to take a different degree. Some people are badly advised to go off and do another degree and then try and transfer from another course into veterinary science. This is not feasible because it is necessary from the beginning to study certain subjects which are exclusive to veterinary science. Examples are veterinary anatomy and ruminant physiology. In addition, the chance of there being extra places is remote. Transfer, therefore, becomes impossible and the only way you could proceed would be to go back and start your veterinary studies at the beginning. Therefore, no one should be advised to take a different course and then try to transfer. However, it is worth noting that Cambridge has been known to make some concessions to students wishing to transfer from mainly medically related degrees. Such students might, because of the Cambridge tripos system, be able to complete a veterinary science degree at the end of six or seven years' study depending upon when the transfer was made. Such students still need to study veterinary physiology and anatomy.

Further reasons why it might prove unwise to do a degree in another subject are that even if you become a graduate in another cognate subject, with an upper second or even a first, your application could be assessed on the basis of your original A levels as well as the subsequent university study. This is done in fairness to the large number of school-leavers applying. A decisive argument for most people is that in nearly all these cases graduates in other subjects would only be admitted on a 'full cost' basis. Some colleges allocate a small number of places to graduates within the Home and EU intake. Tuition fees for these would usually be at full cost fees payable throughout the course. (However, fees at Nottingham and the Royal Veterinary College for home graduates are currently the same as for first-degree students.) There are no scholarships available for graduate applicants, with the possible exception of some of those at Cambridge colleges or which are privately funded.

DEFERRING ENTRY AND TAKING A GAP YEAR

The UCAS system permits you to apply at the start of your upper sixth year for entry a year after completion of your A levels. However, you will be expected to meet the conditions of the offer in the year of application. The majority of veterinary schools now welcome students deciding to postpone their entry on to the course. The most common reasons given by students are the opportunity to travel, study or work abroad, or gain additional relevant experience for the course and profession they seek to enter. The latter reason is the one most likely to influence veterinary schools because many applicants do need to strengthen their range of relevant work experience.

You should be able to explain your plans for the year taken out. Does it involve some animal experience? Those coming from urban areas may find that undertaking a gap year of a relevant nature is slightly more difficult to achieve. It is a good idea to discuss this matter on an informal basis with an admissions tutor and get advice.

A LEVEL PREDICTIONS

As has already been indicated, A level performance (or its equivalent) is not a sole determinant in selection because of the importance of other motivational factors. However, predicted A level performance is an important factor for admissions tutors in sifting through and finding committed candidates likely to meet the stipulated academic level. Final decisions are made when A level results are known.

It is at this point that some rejected applicants will do better than predicted. When the admissions tutors learn that the rejected candidate has achieved top grades and is excellent in other respects, they have been known to change the original rejection to an unconditional acceptance for the following year. Over 100 places are settled each year in this way. Indeed, the majority of entrants to veterinary science courses will have taken a year out, whether they intended this or not.

Those whose grades slip slightly below their conditional offer will usually be considered in August and could be offered entry if places are available. The importance, therefore, of A levels is that once the results are known, the tutors can announce decisions finally taken from within the group of well-motivated and committed pre-selected candidates.

IMPORTANCE OF THE PERSONAL STATEMENT

The personal statement may be the last part of the UCAS application you fill in, but it is certainly the most important and influential. Most of the information you supply via UCAS is a factual summary of what you have achieved, but in the personal statement you have your first chance to give expression, clarity and style to your application and hence bid for a place at veterinary school.

Make sure you plan your answer carefully. Remember that brevity can often produce a better, more directed answer. Word-process the statement first and then cut it down to within the correct number of characters if necessary. Research shows that it is a good idea to structure your response. Consider using subheadings to give clarity for the busy admissions tutor.

Make sure that the following points are covered in your personal statement:

- Why do you want to be a veterinary surgeon? There are many possible reasons and this is where your individuality will show.
- Outline your practical experience. Give prominence to the diverse nature of it, the clinics, farms, stables etc. Mention any specific interesting cases that you witnessed or assisted with.
- You like animals, but how do you respond to people? How did you get on with vets, nurses and the customers? Any teamwork experience?
- Give an indication of your career direction, even if it is tentative at this stage. Show that you have thought about the possibilities.
- Any special achievements or responsibilities connected either with animals or with an outside interest?
- List other activities and interests of a social, cultural or sporting kind. Here is your chance to reveal more about yourself as an individual.

Finally, remember to keep a copy of your personal statement before you pass it on to your referee. The copy will serve to refresh your memory before you are called for interviews.

An example personal statement is shown on the page opposite for illustrative purposes. It shows the way in which an applicant might structure the personal statement.

My determination to study Veterinary Medicine has been reinforced by my work experience with both large and small animals. I find working with animals hugely rewarding and I have always had a strong interest in their care and welfare. Veterinary Medicine would give me further opportunities to pursue my interest in science, and apply my knowledge to tackle a wide variety of problems in diagnosis, treatment and research. Veterinary Medicine combines all aspects that I would look for in a vocation, including working closely with people and working as part of a team. Below is a summary of my work experience to date:

1 week at Glades Veterinary Surgery (small animal)
1 week at Hunters House Veterinary Surgery (mixed practice)
2 weeks at Equine Veterinary Practice
1 week at the Blue Cross
3 weeks at Hayes Park Dairy Farm, including calving
1½ weeks at Crocketts Farm (public), including lambing
2 weeks at Forest Stables
3 years at Slemans Barn Farm (stables)
1 year at Bilbow Stables
1 day at Smith's Abattoir

At Hayes Park, I was able to take an active role in all aspects of calf husbandry and found the hands-on and practical nature of the work very appealing. Working at the farm also highlighted the difficulty farmers have in balancing commercial and welfare aspects in farming. This was particularly evident during the foot-and-mouth crisis where it appeared that many of these problems can be due to commercial pressures, such as ever-decreasing market value of livestock. Whilst working at Crocketts Farm I worked with a variety of animals from rabbits and guinea pigs to zebu and llamas. This work also included lambing, often in front of the general public. I frequently had to answer questions about what was happening and explain my actions. This customer aspect of the work was very satisfying. The time I spent in local veterinary practices allowed me to assist and watch both basic and more complex surgical procedures. I found it fascinating being able to watch an endoscopy being carried out on the oesophagus of a horse and I was able to relate my knowledge of biology to what I was seeing. My equine veterinary experience showed me how I could combine my love of horses with a career in veterinary medicine. I also enjoyed participating in the Vetsim and Vetsix courses.

Interests and Responsibilities
Horse riding (I own a seven-year-old gelding and am actively involved in all aspects of his care and schooling); Duke of Edinburgh (achieved the Bronze and Silver awards and currently completing the Gold award); Manston Drama Club (local theatre group – I played lead in last production); Music (Grade 4 piano, Grade 5 flute and currently working towards Grade 5 theory); School Prefect.

Following my exams, I have arranged to travel to South Africa for three months. I will spend my time teaching in local primary schools for under-privileged children and working in the Simbari game reserve. The game reserve activities include wildlife veterinary work, game monitoring and assisting with guests at the Game Lodge.

REFEREE'S REPORT

After you have completed the declaration, your application is ready to be passed to your referee for completion. They will then send it to UCAS. The referee is usually your head teacher who can draw upon the opinions of the staff and information contained in the school records. However, mature students or graduates for whom school was too long ago for such a reference to be meaningful should approach people who know them well. A good idea is to consider asking someone for whom they have recently worked.

References are an important factor since they provide insight into your character and personality. They can also provide significant confirmation of career aims, achievements and interests. The referee's view of your abilities in terms of analysis, powers of expression and willingness to question things, are the kinds of independent information about you that will have an influence with selectors. Additional information about family circumstances and health problems, which candidates rarely offer about themselves, will also be taken into account.

OTHER SUPPORTING DOCUMEN-TATION

Because work experience in veterinary practices and farms is so important in the selection of applicants for veterinary school, you will be expected to list full details of all such experience. Some veterinary schools will send you a questionnaire asking you to expand on the information you have given about work experience in the UCAS application. Applicants can expect interested veterinary schools to follow up and write on a confidential basis to the veterinary practices and farms where you have worked for additional information about you. This is a good sign as it shows that your application has aroused more than a passing interest.

In essence the veterinary school will ask whether the people you have worked with regard you as a suitable entrant into the veterinary profession. The sorts of things which concern tutors are:

■ General enthusiasm
■ Ability to express yourself clearly

■ Helpfulness
■ Practical ability
■ Attitude to the animals, to customers and to clerical and nursing staff in the practice – in other words, were you a pleasure to have around?

So it is clear that the veterinary school can take steps to get hold of additional information about you. It is also possible for you to help yourself by taking the initiative to gain documentary support. For example, once you have received your UCAS acknowledgement and application number, ask your local vet to write to the veterinary school(s) of your choice (quoting your application number), giving details of the five weeks' work that you did with extra detail on any interesting cases with which you were involved. This information will go into your file and is bound to help, especially if the vet is able to say that he or she 'would like to see this person in veterinary school'.

There are exceptions to this arrangement. For instance, the Royal Veterinary College would prefer that copies of all supporting statements, references and casebooks be brought to your interview rather than sent in advance.

MATURE STUDENTS

In view of the extreme competition it is unrealistic for mature students, at say age 25–30 years old, to expect special treatment. They must usually expect to satisfy the academic entry requirements in the usual way at one recent sitting and must have a good range of practical experience. However, this requirement has been known to be waived in exceptional cases, such as where there might be a mature student displaying strong motivation coupled with academic ability.

Mature applicants should use the personal statement section of the UCAS application to set out their qualifications and work experience. Your objective is to signal to the admissions tutors why they should see you. Your extra maturity and practical experience should show here. If you cannot get all the information in the space allowed, make sure you summarise what you want to get across under the main subheadings. Remember it is very important to show why you want to work with animals and to give details of any relevant work experience of a paid or voluntary nature. If you feel that the space in the personal statement section of the UCAS application did not permit you to do full justice to yourself, it is a good idea to prepare a curriculum vitae or further documentation and send your this direct to the veterinary school with your UCAS application number.

WHAT TO DO IF YOU ARE REJECTED

Generally one of the main reasons for rejection is insufficient practical experience, particularly a lack of farm work. If this is true in your own case, the action you could take is to try to remedy the deficiency between the A level examinations and the publication of the results. All applications are reconsidered after your A level results are known. If your academic results are satisfactory you may be offered a place for the subsequent year.

If rejected but you have reached the necessary academic standard or have narrowly fallen short, you should think carefully before turning away from veterinary science, if that is really what you want to do. There are plenty of cases of people who have persisted and gained the extra practical experience that was needed to tip the scales in their favour. Determination to succeed is a quality that is generally recognised and supported. Think carefully before turning away to take another science subject. In most cases such a move will prove to be a decisive career choice. This is because it is not possible to transfer from another science course into veterinary school. Nor is it easy to take veterinary science as a second Bachelor's degree: graduate applicants have to face stiffer competition and the prospect of having to pay high fees if accepted.

RETAKING A LEVELS

Many unsuccessful candidates decide to do a repeat year and take the examinations again. Before doing this it would be sensible to seek the advice of an admissions tutor. The fact is that not many people doing repeats are made conditional offers unless there are documented extenuating circumstances, such as serious illness. If you are made an offer it will usually be based upon the second attempt and the requirement will probably be raised to achieving grade A in all three subjects. You may get a repeat offer if you have narrowly failed to secure a place on the first try and are excellent in all other respects. However, most candidates who reapply have to take their chance in Clearing after a preliminary rejection.

The truth is that the almost overwhelming pressure of demand by highly motivated and well-qualified candidates is taking its toll on the chances of those repeating A levels. Selection is becoming more stringent, resulting in fewer resitters being successful.

It is possible to improve A level grades by retaking anything between one and six units, depending on how many times the units have been sat and how close you are to the A-grade boundary. It is often sensible to retake AS units as they are easier than the A2 units. To achieve an A grade at A level you need to score 480 UMS marks out of 600, and it does not matter how the 480 is achieved so it makes sense to gain as many of the 'easier' marks as possible. Your retake strategy will depend on how many extra marks you need and which examination board set your papers (which will determine when resits are available). Independent sixth-form colleges are usually happy to advise students about their options.

CASE STUDY

Alice is now studying Veterinary Medicine in London. She was unsuccessful in her first application. 'I really was not prepared well enough for my application. This was my fault rather than my school's, because the school didn't have any experience of veterinary applications. I should have taken the whole process much more seriously. I had wanted to be a vet from the age of about fourteen although probably for the wrong reasons. I loved my pets and like most girls of that age, wanted to own a horse. My school gave me advice about the AS and A levels to choose, and showed me where the prospectuses and university guides were in the careers room. I had an idea that work experience was important but, living in central London, my opportunities were limited. I got a Saturday job in a pet shop, and I hoped that this would be sufficient. I got eight A or A* grades at GCSE and I was predicted A grades in all my A level subjects, and I was very surprised when I was rejected by all four vet schools. It was only at that point that I realised how serious I was about becoming a vet.

'I discussed the situation with my family and they agreed to me taking a gap year and reapplying. This time I did my research. I arranged a variety of work experience placements, using the vet school prospectuses and web sites to guide me as to what was needed. I went to open days and tried to talk to as many students as possible about their applications in order to make sure I was as well-prepared as they had been. I also made a point of reading as widely as possible about veterinary-related issues in preparation for the interview. To be honest, if I had got an interview the first time I almost certainly would have been rejected because I would not have been able to answer most of the questions convincingly. In retrospect, being rejected in my first application was a good thing, because it helped me to realise how committed I needed to be in order to be successful as a vet.'

5

THE INTERVIEW

When the veterinary schools have received the UCAS applications, they will sift through them and decide who to call for interview. Only approximately one in three applicants to each institution will get an interview, but this can vary from year to year and between universities.

TIMING

The timing of interviews can be anywhere from November to March, so some candidates have to wait some time before getting their interview, and because of this timescale some candidates will get a late decision. The Cambridge colleges usually conduct their interviews in December, along with those for other courses at the university.

THE PURPOSE OF THE INTERVIEW

The interview is designed to find out more about you. In particular, the interviewers (possibly a panel) will want to satisfy themselves about your motivation and the extent of your commitment to becoming a qualified veterinary surgeon. Have you an appropriate attitude towards animal welfare? Are you reasonably well informed about the implications of embarking on a veterinary career? Are you a mature person possessing a balanced outlook on life?

Are they going to be satisfied that you have the ability to cope with the pace of what is generally acknowledged to be a long and demanding course?

To help them they will have your UCAS application, the head teacher's reference and any supporting statements made by veterinary practitioners or people for whom you have worked. They will already have a good idea of your academic ability or you would not be at the interview in the first place.

PREPARATION

Experience shows that personal qualities are just as important as academic ability, perhaps more so. The way you come across will be influenced by how confident you are. This does not mean being over-confident. Many people believe that they can get through interviews by thinking on their feet and taking each question as it comes. This is probably an unwise attitude. Good preparation holds the key. By being well informed on a variety of issues you will be able to formulate answers to most questions. There will always be the unexpected question for which no amount of preparation can get you ready, but you can minimise the chance of this happening.

Confidence based on good preparation is the best kind. It is not of the puffed-up variety that can soon be punctured by searching questions. While it is true that the interviewers will want to put you at your ease and will try to make the atmosphere informal and friendly, there is no doubt that for you there will be some tension in the situation. Think positively – this may be no bad thing; many of us perform better when we are on our toes.

Some schools will be able to offer you a mock interview. Sometimes they can arrange for a person from outside the school to give the interview which can help to give a realistic feel to it. If you are not sure about whether this facility is available, ask your school careers department. They will be keen to help if they can.

Do you know anyone, student or staff, connected with one of the veterinary schools? If you do, ask for their advice. They may be able to give you an idea of what to expect.

Start your preparation by looking at your copy of the personal statement you submitted to UCAS. This is the most important part of your UCAS application and it should tell the interviewers a lot about you as a person, your work experience, your interests and skills. Many of the questions they will ask will be prompted by what you have written in it. The questions will most likely begin with those designed to put you at your ease. As the interview proceeds you should expect them to become more searching. Try practising your answers to questions like these:

Question: *Did you have any trouble getting here?*
Comment: This is the sort of friendly question meant to get you started. Do not spend too long on it, take the opportunity to be social, try to get relaxed and smile.

Question: *Have you visited here before?*
Comment: Did you go to the open day? If so, this is the moment to mention the fact. The interviewer will almost certainly follow up and ask what you thought of it. The faculty probably invested a lot of time and work in preparing it, so go easy on criticism! However, you should be prepared to say what you found was helpful and informative. It is then easier to make an additional constructive criticism. Bear in mind that the interviewers will expect you to have done your homework. If you hope to spend the next five or six years of your life at that institution, you should certainly have made efforts to see whether it is the right place for you. Although your choice is limited to four out of seven veterinary schools, you still have a choice to make. If you answer, 'No, but I've heard that you have a good reputation,' you are hardly likely to convince them that you really want to go there. Similarly, answering, 'No, but I think that all of the veterinary schools are pretty similar,' will not enhance your chances.

Question: *What did you think of our brochure?*
Comment: This is an alternative opening question on which you may have an opinion. Some veterinary schools, like London, have their own brochure; others have their entries in the main prospectus. Be prepared, show that you have at least read it and have an opinion. You could

say 'I thought that it was very informative about the structure of the course, and I particularly liked the case histories of your students – they made me realise that students in a similar situation to me can get a place.' Hopefully, this will lead to a question which will allow you to talk about your experience.

Question: *How do you think you are doing with your A levels?*
Comment: This is not a time for modesty. You would not be having this interview if your school had not predicted you good results. You should be sounding optimistic while at the same time indicating that you are working hard. They may also be interested to learn which are your favourite subjects so be ready for a follow-up question along those lines. If you have a good set of AS results, you could mention them at this point. You could also talk about a Biology project which was relevant to veterinary science. As with the two previous examples, your aim should be to steer these rather boring questions towards topic areas that you have prepared and which will show you in the strongest light.

Question: *What do you think of the TV programmes about vets?*
Comment: There are so many of them, where do you start? Such programmes could be good or bad for the professional standing of the vet. They make good television, especially when they show the animals and the caring 'honest broker' role of the vet between animals and mankind. They also almost universally present vets as likeable people. On the other hand you could argue that veterinary science is undermined when the programmes degenerate into 'soaps', with a portrayal of young vets whose work is an easy or incidental part of their lives. In your answer show that you have thought about TV's influence.

Question: *Why do you want to study veterinary science?*
Comment: The direction of the interview can change quite suddenly. Be ready for the switch in questioning; the answer will bring into focus your attitude to animals, the range of your work experience, those important manual skills, and your commitment to all the hard work entailed

in studying to become a qualified professional veterinary surgeon admitted to the Register of the Royal College of Veterinary Surgeons. This is your opportunity, if you have not already done so, to mention your work experience, and to emphasise how your determination to become a vet increased as a result. This is an important question and needs a full answer but keep your reply to under two minutes. Practise this. Remember that research findings show that if you exceed two minutes you risk boring your listeners.

Question: *Why do you want to come to this veterinary school?*
Comment: This is a natural follow-up question, so be prepared for it. The answer is personal to you; you may want to go to a new area of the country or you may know the area well because of relatives. Your local vet may have recommended this particular veterinary school to you. The reputation of the school may have impressed you because of some particular speciality in which you are also interested. There could be several reasons.

Question: *Tell us something about your work experience with animals.*
Comment: This is one of the big questions of the interview. It would be surprising if the interviewers do not already have feedback from where you have been working. The interviewers will know what happens in a veterinary practice or on a farm, so lists of things that you saw or did will not shed any light on your suitability for the profession. Instead, concentrate on your reactions to the experience. Did you enjoy it? Were there any interesting or unusual cases that stick in your memory? Does any of your enthusiasm show? Do you indicate any respect and sympathy for the animals? And what about the people – did you get on with them? The key phrases here are, 'For example, when I ...' and 'For instance, I was able to ...'

Question: *What are the main things you learned from your work experience?*
Comment: This is the typical follow-up question that gives you a chance to summarise and underline your impressions. You could try to indicate the varied nature of your experience, the different types of practice or farms

you saw. There is also the business side of working with animals for which you may not originally have been prepared. Maybe you were astonished at the responsibilities of the veterinary nurses. Be prepared to intrigue your listeners. A related question is, 'From your work experience, what do you think are the qualities necessary to be a successful vet?' Rather than answering, 'Stamina, communication, physical fitness, problem-solving … [and so on]', bring in examples of things that you saw. For example: 'The ability to solve problems. For instance, when I accompanied a vet to a riding school, it was clear that one of the horses was very distressed, but it was unclear why …' and then go on to explain the steps involved in the diagnosis and treatment.

Question: *Have you ever felt frightened of animals?*
Comment: Vets shouldn't be frightened of animals, particularly small ones! However, honesty compels most of us to admit that we have at times and in certain situations felt vulnerable to a kick or bite. Explain the situation and what was said at the time – vets are noted for their humour!

Question: *What do you think of rearing animals for meat?*
Comment: This type of question might be asked because it checks on your motivation. Perhaps you should start by looking at it from the animal viewpoint. Animals should be kept well with good standards of husbandry and eventually slaughtered humanely. Of course, the animal does not know the reason for its being slaughtered, but you do. Some of your future clients may be farmers who make their living from supplying meat or poultry – what is your reaction? If you oppose meat, you should be honest but make it clear that you would be able to remain professional.

Question: *How do you feel about cruelty to animals?*
Comment: With the strong interest in and liking for animals that you would expect from all veterinary students, they will be watching your reaction. This is a question that you should expect and your response, while putting animal welfare first, should be strong and well reasoned rather than too emotional. What would you do if

you thought a farmer was acting in a cruel way to some of his livestock? Go to the police straight away? Talk over the difficulty with a colleague? Threaten the farmer by mentioning that you might bring in the RSPCA? The interviewers are not expecting you to come up with a perfect answer but rather to show that you are capable of coming up with a well-balanced and reasoned solution.

TOPICAL AND CONTROVERSIAL ISSUES

Most interviews last only 15–20 minutes so there may not be time for questions of a more topical or controversial nature. Nevertheless it may be worth you investing a little thought into how you might sketch out an answer to questions covering one or more of the following issues, each of which will be outlined in the next chapter of this book:

- Bovine spongiform encephalopathy (BSE)
- Bird flu
- Foot-and-mouth disease
- Intensive farming
- Tuberculosis and badgers
- Fox hunting
- Fall of dairy prices
- Dangerous Dogs Act
- Bluetongue disease
- Animal testing

Remember, most of the time there is no right or wrong answer when questioned on issues such as these. It is really a case of demonstrating your understanding of an issue, your quality of judgement and your ability to discuss the issue clearly, logically and succinctly. A burst of enthusiasm and conviction won't do any harm either!

IMPORTANCE OF THE INTERVIEW

These are just a few of the possible questions and issues that you might expect to come up at a selection interview for entry to veterinary school. To be called for interview is a positive sign as it indicates that your application is being considered and a good interview can lead to an offer. Another reason for trying to do well at the interview stage is that those candidates whose grades fall just below that required in their conditional offers are always reconsidered. If places are available, a good interview performance could tip the balance in your favour.

DEMEANOUR

Most candidates will do their best to prepare well for the interview by anticipating likely questions. However, very few candidates realise that the visual impression they are creating will count for as much as their verbal answers to questions. It is a bit like the old saying 'It's not what you say but the way that you say it'!

Admissions tutors are unlikely to admit that they are going to be influenced by appearance and body language, but they are only human. There is bound to be subjectivity involved. What can you do about it? Try to look your best and try to be as relaxed as possible in what will seem to be a fairly tense situation. Here are a few points to watch.

BODY LANGUAGE

When you first enter the room, smile and give a firm handshake. Veterinary schools are friendly places and like to exude informality.

Sit comfortably and reasonably upright, leaning forward slightly. This position makes you look and feel alert. Try not to be so tense that you are crouching forward giving an impression of a panther about to spring. Do not go to the other extreme of leaning back and looking irritatingly self-assured. Where do you put your hands during the interview? Try resting one on top of the other over your lap. Alternatively let each hand rest by your side. It is not a good idea to have your arms folded – it looks as though you are shutting the interviewer out!

Speak clearly and deliberately. Do not rush things. When people are nervous they tend to speed up which makes it harder for the listener. Make eye contact by looking at the person who asked you the question. If it is a panel interview let your glance take in others at the table, make them feel that they are included. You should certainly have at least one mock interview if available, which, if possible, should be recorded on video so that you can see how you come across. You will then be able to spot any mannerisms, such as touching your head or cracking your knuckles, that might distract the interviewers.

YOUR APPEARANCE

Look your best. This does not mean that you should appear like a tailor's dummy. Wear clothes which are smart, not showy, and in which you feel comfortable. Pay attention to details like polishing your shoes and washing your hair.

CASE STUDY

'Most students who apply to become vets worry more about the interview than about the UCAS application, but what they should realise is that once you get to the interview stage you have a very good chance of being offered a place.' Peter has just started his first year at Bristol, and received two offers when he applied. Peter took lots of advice from veterinary students and practising vets beforehand, many of whom emphasised that the interview was far less stressful than applicants imagine.

Peter went into the interview feeling nervous but also reasonably confident that he would be offered a place: 'I wasn't being arrogant in thinking I would get a place – it was because I had done lots of preparation. I knew that my work experience would probably be the main feature of the interview and I had kept a diary of all the things I did and saw. During my work experience I pestered the farmers and vets all the time with questions and at the end of each day I wrote down what they had said. I felt pretty sure that I could show the interviewers that I was genuinely interested in veterinary medicine.

'Before the interviews, I revised from my diaries in the same way I would revise for an exam. I also had some practice interviews with my school. At my real interviews, I was asked some general questions about the qualities a vet needs and I made sure I always illustrated these with examples of things I had actually seen or spoken about with the vets I worked with. In some ways I was over-prepared because I knew that only a fraction of what I had prepared would come up, but that also meant that I felt confident when I went into the interview.

'One of my friends was rejected and the feedback that he got after the interview (our school telephoned the vet school to find out why he had been rejected) was that he did not seem sufficiently interested in what he had encountered in his work experience – so I was extremely glad that I had prepared properly. In both interviews, the people there were friendly and helpful, encouraging me and seeming to be interested in what I said. The time passed very quickly, though, and I was glad I was able to bring in my work experience very early in the interview.'

6

RECENT AND CURRENT ISSUES

You must aim to keep up to date with recent and new developments which affect the veterinary profession. The best sources of these are the broadsheet newspapers and internet news websites. As well as the news sections, the health sections contain articles that will be of interest. Your interviewer will want to find out whether you are genuinely interested in the profession, and one way to test this is to investigate your awareness and appreciation of important issues; after all, if you are planning to devote the next 40 or so years of your life to veterinary science, you ought to be interested in issues that affect the profession.

Read a newspaper every day, cut out or photocopy articles of interest, and keep them in a scrapbook so that you can revise before your interview. You will also find the Department for Environment, Food and Rural Affairs website (www.defra.gov.uk) extremely helpful. Other useful websites are listed in Chapter 8.

Ten issues to bear in mind are all outlined and explained in detail below. Being able to provide right or wrong answers relating to each is not really the issue (if you'll excuse the pun!). It is really a case of knowing as much as you can about things which are important to the veterinary profession. It is about building up a healthy stock of information and knowledge, one of the major benefits of which will be the confidence you feel in discussing such issues should they come up at interview.

BSE

Bovine spongiform encephalopathy (BSE) was first identified in 1986, although it is possible that it had been known about since 1983. It is a neurological disease that affects the brains of cattle, and is similar to scrapie, a disease of sheep that has been known about since the 18th century. In 1988, the government's working party, chaired by Sir Richard Southwood, stated that there was minimal risk to humans since, as scrapie was known not to spread to humans, neither would BSE. It is believed that BSE originated in cattle as a result of the practice of using the remains of diseased sheep as part of high-protein cattle feed in an attempt to increase milk yields. In 1989, the government recommended that specific offals – such as the brain and the spleen – should be discarded rather than allowed to enter the food chain, and that diseased cattle should be incinerated. In the early 1990s, the increased incidence of CJD – a disease similar to BSE that affects humans – caused scientists to look at the possibility that the disease had jumped species. At about the same time, scientists found increasing evidence of transmission between species following experiments involving mice, pigs and cats. By 1993, there were over 800 new cases of BSE a week, despite the ban on animal feed containing specified offals. It became clear that the increase in the cases of CJD was related to the rise in BSE, and that it was likely that millions of infected cattle had been eaten before the symptoms appeared. In 1996, the EU banned the export of cattle, beef and beef products that originated in the UK. In 1997, the government set up a public inquiry, chaired by Lord Phillips. The findings were released in October 2000. Details can be found on the inquiry website (www.bseinquiry.gov.uk). The total number of confirmed cases of BSE in Great Britain since 1986 is estimated to be about 183,000. There has been an overall decline in the epidemic in recent years, with confirmed cases now falling by around 50% each year.

The BSE problem raised a number of issues concerning farming and food safety. In retrospect, the decision to allow the remains of diseased animals to be incorporated into feed for herbivores seems to be misguided, at the very least. The problem with BSE is that the infecting agent, the prion (a previously unknown pathogen composed of proteins) was able to survive the treatments used to destroy bacteria and viruses. If any good has come out of the problem, it is that we are now much more aware of food safety. In April 2000, the government established the Food Standards Agency, created to 'protect public health from risks which may arise in connection with the consumption of food, and otherwise to protect the interests of consumers in relation to food'. Although it has been established by the government, it has the independence to publish any advice that it gives the government, avoiding the accusations of cover-ups and secrecy levelled at the government over the BSE affair.

In March 2006, EU veterinary experts agreed unanimously today to lift the ban on British beef exports, imposed ten years earlier to prevent the spread of mad cow disease. The EU's standing committee on the food chain and animal health said that the UK had fulfilled all the conditions for the ban to end. The closure of export markets cost the British beef industry around £675 million.

BIRD FLU

Avian flu was thought only to infect birds until the first human cases were seen in Hong Kong in 1997. Birds excrete the virus in their faeces, which dries and becomes pulverised, and is then inhaled. Humans can catch the disease through close contact with live infected birds. Symptoms are similar to other types of flu – fever, malaise, sore throat and coughing. People can also develop conjunctivitis. All 18 people infected in 1997 had been in close contact with live birds in markets or on farms.

Countries known to have been infected by the disease include Cambodia, Indonesia, South Korea, China, Japan, Thailand, Vietnam and Hong Kong. Furthermore, since January 2004, human cases of avian influenza have been reported in Asia, Africa, the Pacific, Europe and the Near East. Avian flu has been seen to have a high fatality rate in humans. In 1997, six out of the 18 people who were infected died. In an outbreak in 2004, there were over 20 confirmed deaths.

There are 15 different strains of the virus. It is the H5N1 strain which is infecting humans and causing high death rates. Even within the H5N1 strain, however, variations are seen, and slightly different strains are being seen in the different countries where there have been outbreaks of the disease.

The H5N1 virus that emerged in Asia in 2003 continues to evolve and may adapt so that other mammals may be susceptible to infection as well. Moreover, it is likely that H5N1 infection among birds has become endemic in certain areas and that human infections resulting from direct contact with infected poultry and/or wild birds will continue to occur. So far, the spread of H5N1 virus from person to person has been rare and limited.

Patients suffering from avian flu can be treated with antiviral drugs whilst researchers continue to work to develop a vaccine. In 2004, the European Union announced that it was considering a precautionary ban on the importation of poultry meat and products from Thailand. At the same time, millions of birds were culled in an attempt to stop the spread of the disease among birds, which would in turn stop it being passed on to humans.

Currently, in 2006, there is a ban on the importation of birds and bird products from H5N1-affected countries. The regulation states that no person may import or attempt to import any birds, whether dead or alive, or any products derived from birds (including hatching eggs), from the specified countries.

In January 2006, two children from the eastern Turkish town of Dogubeyazit, whose family kept poultry at their home, died having contracted the virulent H5N1 strain. Three months later, in the Scottish town of Fife, tests confirmed that a swan found dead there also died from the deadly H5N1 strain of the avian flu virus. The discovery made Britain the 14th country in Europe to have the disease in its territory.

At the time of going to press, in February 2007, there had just been a major outbreak on a turkey farm in Suffolk.

FOOT-AND-MOUTH DISEASE

The outbreak of foot-and-mouth disease (FMD) that occurred in February 2001 was the first in the UK for 20 years. Between February and September, 2030 cases occurred. The last major outbreak was in 1967, during which about half a million animals were slaughtered. Before the re-emergence of the disease, in a new and highly virulent form, it had been thought that FMD had been eradicated from Western Europe. The latest form of the virus seems to have originated in Asia, and could have been brought into the UK in a number of ways. Something as trivial as a discarded sandwich containing meat from an infected source — brought into the country by, for example, a tourist — could have been incorporated into pigswill (pig food made from waste food) and then passed on to animals from other farms at a livestock sale. The BSE problem led to greater regulation over abattoirs, which resulted in the closure of many smaller abattoirs. Animals destined for slaughter now have to travel greater distances and the possibility of FMD being passed to other animals is, as a consequence, greater.

The UK was declared foot-and-mouth free on 14 January 2002, almost a year after the first reported case. More than four million animals, from over 7000 farms, were slaughtered during this period. The last recorded case occurred at the end of September 2001. The official report highlighted the lack of speed with which the government acted and commented on the fact that the understaffed State Veterinary Service was unable to effectively monitor the disease. The disease took a month to diagnose and by the time animal movement was halted, over 20,000 infected sheep had spread the virus across the UK.

FMD is endemic in parts of Asia, Africa and South America with sporadic outbreaks in disease-free areas. Countries affected by FMD within the last two years include Afghanistan, Bhutan, Iran, Lebanon, Peru, South Africa, the United Arab Emirates and Vietnam. There have been no outbreaks of the disease in the EU since the 2001 outbreak which affected not only the UK but also Ireland, France and the Netherlands.

A Royal Society report recommended that vaccination – commonly used in a number of countries – should be a weapon in any future outbreaks. Vaccination is unpopular with some meat exporters since it is difficult to distinguish between animals that have been vaccinated and those that have the disease, and for this reason many FMD-free countries ban the import of vaccinated cattle.

FMD is a viral disease that affects cattle, pigs, sheep, goats and deer. Hedgehogs and rats (and elephants!) can also become infected, and people, cats, dogs and game animals can carry infected material. The virus can be transferred by saliva, milk, dung and the breath of infected animals, and also can become airborne – where it can travel large distances, perhaps as much as 150 miles. A vehicle that has driven through dung from an infected animal can carry the virus to other farms on its tyres. It is more contagious than any other animal disease, and the mortality rate amongst young animals is high.

The role of the veterinary surgeon in a suspected outbreak of foot-and-mouth disease is not a pleasant one. If the existence of the disease is confirmed, the vet must make arrangements with Defra to ensure that all animals on the farm (and possibly on neighbouring farms) are slaughtered and then incinerated. For economic reasons, there is no question of the vet being allowed to try to treat infected animals.

There has only been one recorded case of FMD in a human being in Great Britain and that was in 1966. The general effects of the disease in that case were similar to influenza with some blisters. It is a mild short-lived, self-limiting disease. The Food Standards Agency have advised that the disease in animals has no implications for the human food chain.

INTENSIVE FARMING

Prominent features of the British diet are meat and dairy products. Although carbohydrates (such as pasta and rice) are providing a greater proportion of our diets than they did ten years ago, we still eat protein in higher quantities than is consumed by our Southern European neighbours. We also demand cheap food. The meat, poultry, dairy and egg industries are faced with a choice – to use technological methods in order to keep the price of their products as low as possible, or to allow the animals that they farm to lead more 'natural' lives which would necessarily reduce yields and increase costs. The use of drugs, hormones and chemicals is almost universal in farming (except within the organic farming movement), as are methods to control the movement of livestock by the use of pens, cages or stalls. The veterinary profession is faced with a number of difficult decisions. It has to balance the pressure to produce cheap food with its primary aim of maintaining and improving animal welfare. An example of this is the use of antibiotics. Antibiotics are used in farming to treat sick animals. However, they are also used to protect healthy animals against the diseases associated with intensive farming and as growth promoters. The Soil Association reports that about 1225 tons of antibiotics are used each year in the UK, over 60% of which are used for farm animals or by vets. The problem with antibiotics is that bacteria become resistant to them, and overuse of antibiotics in animals has these serious effects:

■ Resistant strains of bacteria, such as salmonella and E coli, can be passed on to humans, causing illness and, in extreme cases, death.
■ Bacteria can develop resistance to the drugs that are used to treat serious illness in humans.

Other issues that concern the veterinary profession include:

■ The welfare of live farm animals that are exported for slaughter
■ Battery farming of poultry
■ The use of growth hormones
■ Humane killing of farm animals in abattoirs.

The Protection of Animals Act (1911) contains the general law relating to the suffering of animals, and agricultural livestock is also protected by more recent legislation. New regulations came into force in August 2000, incorporating EU law. The regulations cover laying hens, poultry, calves, cattle, pigs and rabbits. More specifically, the EU has banned the veal crate from 2007 and the traditional battery cage from 2012. Details of the regulations can be found on the Defra website (the address is in Chapter 8).

TUBERCULOSIS AND BADGERS

Bovine tuberculosis (bTB) is a serious disease in cattle. Although the risks of tuberculosis spreading to humans through milk or meat are small, it can be transmitted through other means, particularly to farm workers who have direct contact with the animals. The number of cattle slaughtered because of TB increased from 599 in 1986 to 22,570 in 2004. Furthermore, the National Farmers' Union has estimated that the cost to British farming could easily reach £150 million by 2010. There is uncertainty about the cause of the spread of bTB in cattle, but many people believe that it is passed on by badgers – a protected species. There is widespread support within the farming community for the culling of badgers, but this is opposed by wildlife and conservation groups. In 1998 the government set up a badger-culling trial as well as taking steps to test the carcasses of badgers killed on the roads (about 50,000 every year) in order to try to find out more about the causes of the disease in cattle. However, the results were inconclusive, and the two opposing sides in the argument are still at loggerheads: the fundamental question remains unanswered – is bTB spread from badgers to cattle, from cattle to badgers, or is other wildlife involved?

In November 2004 the government introduced enhanced testing and control measures to help improve the detection of bTB, so that action could be taken quickly to prevent the spread of the disease. A ten-year government strategic framework for the sustainable control of bovine tuberculosis in Great Britain was published in March 2005. Through this framework, the government aims to bring about a sustainable improvement in control of bTB by 2015.

In December 2005, the government also announced pre-movement testing in England and Wales to help reduce the risk of bTB spreading between herds.

According to recent data, there was a reduction in the number of new bTB incidents in 2005 and again in 2006. Despite this reduction, however, levels of bTB remain high in comparison with other EU countries.

FOX HUNTING

Most people have a view on the issue of hunting with hounds. Prior to the Hunting Act of 2004, there were those, on the one hand, who argued that fox hunting was an integral part of rural life, a countryside tradition; that foxes killed farm animals and therefore needed to be controlled, that thousands of rural jobs would be lost if it were banned and that a ban on fox hunting would lead to a ban on other pastimes, like shooting and fishing. On the other hand, many people believed that it was a cruel and unnecessary way to control foxes, claiming that around 20,000 foxes were killed every year and that about half that number of hunting dogs were also killed taking part in the sport. Animal rights activists believed it was immoral to chase and kill animals for the sake of sport.

The Hunting Act of 2004, which banned fox hunting in England and Wales, took effect in February 2005. The Act makes it an offence to hunt a wild mammal with a dog. Nevertheless, some forms of hunting are exempt, including using no more than two dogs to flush out a mammal to be shot.

Controversy on what is a very emotive subject therefore still remains. On the first anniversary of the ban, in

February 2006, hunt supporters called for the Act to be repealed whilst the League Against Cruel Sports accused 33 hunts of repeatedly breaching the law.

For opposing sides of an argument which continues to be pursued, you should investigate the websites hosted by the League Against Cruel Sports (www.league.uk.com) and the Countryside Alliance (www.countryside-alliance.org).

FALL OF DAIRY PRICES

The UK is the ninth largest milk producer in the world and the third largest in Europe. Although largely (90%) self-sufficient in milk, the UK participates in a significant trade in milk production. Nevertheless, farmers' unions are warning that the UK dairy industry is facing meltdown unless a national dairy body is established that can regulate farmgate milk prices.

Milk prices have been low for a number of years and this has been reflected in dairy farm incomes. As a result of the reform of the Common Agricultural Policy (CAP), prices are expected to fall further. Of additional concern to farmers is the fact that some sectors of the supply chain, for example supermarkets, are earning far greater profits than others. As a consequence, some dairy farmers are leaving the industry. The Dairy Supply Chain Forum is working hard to understand why these farmers are leaving. Whilst it is likely that profitability will be an important factor, there are also issues such as succession and possibilities for diversification which need to be considered. One report has suggested that there might be a more significant downturn in production than previously thought, citing the possibility that total UK output may fall by a billion litres in 2007–8.

In an open letter to the Prime Minister, in September 2006, one farm business consultant, David Hughes, referred to the plight of UK dairy farmers as follows:

> *Today UK milk producers receive approximately 10 pence per pint for milk that costs 11.5 pence per pint to produce. The same milk retails for at least 27 pence per pint in the major supermarkets or up to 48 pence per pint on the doorstep. Production costs have been pared to the bone and there is little*

or nothing that family farms can do to achieve further savings.
Put simply, the balance of power within the supply chain is
weighted entirely in favour of the large retailers, with a rela-
tively weak processing sector competing to meet their demands.
The individual milk producer has no bargaining power at all.
If society chooses to ignore this gross imbalance of power we
will rapidly witness the demise of the family-run dairy farm.
They will be replaced by a small number of industrial milk
factories that will contribute nothing to our countryside. Worse
still, we could end up importing our entire milk supply with
all the attendant strategic risks and environmental damage
caused by increased food miles.

DANGEROUS DOGS ACT

The Dangerous Dogs Act, which was introduced in 1991,
banned the ownership, breeding, sale and exchange and
advertising for sale of specified types of fighting dogs. The
dogs covered by the ban included the pit bull terrier. The
Act was amended in 1997, one of the effects of which was
to lift the mandatory destruction orders that courts
applied to dogs found to be of those types listed in the
Act. It is now possible, therefore, for prohibited dogs to
be added to the Index of Exempted Dogs but only at the
direction of a court and only if the necessary conditions
are met (tattooing, microchipping etc). No owner may
apply to have their dog added to the index – it is entirely
a matter for the courts to decide upon. The maximum
penalty for illegal possession of a prohibited dog is a fine
of £5000 and/or 6 months' imprisonment.

Should this issue arise at interview, it is important to
demonstrate that you are aware that vicious attacks by
certain breeds of unmuzzled dogs on children and adults
led to the Act requiring owners to register such dogs with
the police and keep them muzzled. For the qualified vet,
controversy might arise if they are called upon to destroy,
for example, an unmuzzled pit bull terrier before it has
committed an offence. Is such action contrary to the professional oath of a veterinary surgeon? (Privately, many
vets say that the Act is unworkable.) If you take a view on
this in an interview you will get credit for at least
knowing about the law, whether the interviewer agrees
with your conclusion or not.

BLUETONGUE DISEASE

Bluetongue is an insect-borne viral disease to which all species of ruminants are susceptible, although sheep are most severely affected. It is characterised by changes to the mucous linings of the mouth and nose and the coronary band of the foot. It was first described in South Africa but has since been recognised in most countries in the tropics and sub-tropics. Since 1999, there have been widespread outbreaks in Greece, Italy, Corsica and the Balearic Islands. Cases have also occurred in Bulgaria, Croatia, Macedonia and Serbia. It appears that the virus has spread from both Turkey and north Africa. One possible reason for the changing pattern of bluetongue disease in the Mediterranean region is climate changes. Further changes could lead to the disease spreading northward. Bluetongue has, however, never been recorded in the UK.

The clinical signs can vary from inapparent to mild or severe, depending on the virus strain and the breed of sheep involved. Deaths of sheep in a flock may reach as high as 70 per cent. Animals that survive the disease will lose condition with a reduction in meat and wool production.

Over recent months, bluetongue has been found in the Netherlands, Belgium, parts of western Germany and areas of northern France. There is a 150 km restriction zone in place around each of the infected premises, meaning that all of Belgium, the Netherlands and Luxembourg, and parts of western Germany and northern France are under restrictions. In the restriction zone, rules apply to movement of ruminants, export of animals is prohibited and all animals on premises within this zone have to be identified and checked for bluetongue.

ANIMAL TESTING

Almost all of the drugs used to treat us have been tested on animals. Without rigorous and controlled testing there are significant health risks associated with the use of new medicines. In many cases, the long-term or side effects of drugs can be more serious than the illness itself, and testing is therefore essential. Lord Winston, who pioneered in-vitro fertilisation and who found wider publicity through his BBC TV series *The Human Body*, in response to a report by the Lords Select Committee on Science and Technology, was quoted in the *Independent* as saying, 'Perceived pressure may persuade people to go down a route which is not going to promote human welfare. We have a major job – animal research is essential for human welfare. Every drug we use is based on it. Without it those drugs would be unsafe.'

Each year inside British laboratories, approximately three million animals are experimented on. British law requires that any new drug must be tested on at least two different species of live mammal. One must be a large non-rodent. UK regulations are considered some of the most rigorous in the world – the Animals Act of 1986 insists that no animal experiments be conducted if there is a realistic alternative.

The debate on animal testing has become a high-profile one because of the activities of animal rights groups. Although the majority of animal rights groups campaign peacefully, the newspapers have given a good deal of publicity to a number of attacks on research laboratories. Huntingdon Life Sciences, a 50-year-old product development company, has been at the forefront of recent controversy over animal testing. The company claims that it works with a variety of resources, including pharmaceuticals and veterinary products, to help its manufacturers develop safer goods for the market. Some of its opponents claim that HLS kills 500 animals a day in tests for products such as weed killer, food colourings and drugs. In April 2003, HLS won a High Court injunction preventing protesters going within 50 yards of the homes of staff. In the same month activists held protests at three colleges of Cambridge University against the proposal for a primate experimentation laboratory at Girton College. Oxford University, like HLS, sought to obtain an injunction against animal rights protesters following opposition to a new research laboratory. Like HLS, Oxford was also successful. Protests and demonstrations, however, continue to this day.

Opposition to animal testing is centred on the idea that if animals are similar enough to us for test results to be meaningful, then they are too similar to be experimented upon. Conversely, drugs tested on animals have also gone on to have devastating effects on humans. Examples are the drug thalidomide and the trial in March 2006 which caused six men to have multiple organ failure. Campaigners argue that there are alternative methods of testing that do not involve animals. Many of these methods are, they say, also cheaper, quicker and more effective. These include:

- Culture of human cells. This is already used in research into cancer, Parkinson's disease and AIDS
- Molecular methods, including DNA analysis
- Use of micro-organisms
- Computer modelling
- Use of human volunteers.

CASE STUDY

Ellen applied to study veterinary medicine/science last year, and received one offer. She is now in her first year at Liverpool. In the year leading up to her application, Ellen began to worry about the level of interest in veterinary-related issues required for an interview. 'Some of my friends told me to read university text books and veterinary journals in order to make sure I could impress the interviewers, but then a veterinary student at Liverpool, a friend of my brother, advised me not to try to be too scientific in my answers – he said that the interviewers would not expect me to know very advanced or technical things about veterinary medicine, because that is what you go to university to learn! He told me that trying to pretend I understood advanced things was the best way to get rejected, and that knowing about the practical aspects of being a vet was far more helpful in an interview.

'I did as much research on current issues as I could. I spent a lot of time on the internet, trying to use the BBC website as a starting point and then using their links, to find about BSE, bird flu, foot-and-mouth disease, new treatments and similar topics. I knew that I wouldn't be able to know everything about every new issue, change in the law, or treatment, but that having a reasonable knowledge about the most obvious current things was important. In my interview, I was asked a question about the spread of infectious diseases amongst farm animals and so I was able to use what I had learnt about foot-and-mouth as an example. Probably the most useful preparation for me was just talking to people. I did some work experience every Saturday with a local vet and he chatted to me about what he had been doing during the week, and about new developments. Talking to him was much more helpful to me than trying to read about these things because if I didn't understand something I was able to ask him.

'One of the things that came across very strongly was how quickly and often the law or government guidelines for farmers change. This was a constant source of complaint amongst the farmers he dealt with. Although I didn't always understand the issues fully, it gave me an idea of an aspect of veterinary medicine that I hadn't anticipated. In my interview I was asked about some of the negative things about being a vet and I was able to talk about this. The interviewers seemed to like the fact that I had discussed these things with a vet – a sign of my interest and commitment.'

7

CAREER PATHS

There may be hidden expenses In training to be a vet but at least you can reflect, with some optimism, that a degree in veterinary science is going to result in a professional qualification and a job. The vast majority of veterinary surgeons, over 80% of the total at work, are in practice in the UK. There is currently a real shortage of vets. A glance through the pages of the Veterinary Record will confirm the strong demand for the newly qualified vet to go into practice.

The universities' first destination statistics show that nearly all graduates begin their careers in practice, but such is the great variety of opportunity in this profession that career change and divergence can and does occur. Graduates are employed in the government service dealing with investigation, control and eradication of diseases. There are also opportunities for veterinary scientists to become engaged in university teaching and research establishments at home and abroad.

If you start in general practice, there is the chance to move into different types of practice. The trend is towards small-animal practices. There is also more opportunity to work with horses – now seen as an important part of the growing leisure industry.

WORKING IN PRACTICE

It is clear that farm animal practice is seeing a dramatic fall in business and is having to diversify. This trend, evident over the last 20–30 years, is accelerating dramatically for a variety of reasons – the uneconomic structure of much of the farm economy and the tendency for farmers to treat simple problems themselves being the most significant factors. Even mixed practices dealing with farm animals as well as small companion animals like cats and dogs are becoming less common.

The size of practices varies a great deal. Some are small, the average size is three or four vets working together, and a few are much larger. Some are incredibly busy, while others may manage to convey a less rushed atmosphere whilst being equally hardworking.

NEW TRENDS

Membership of the EU has brought a new source of income into general practice. This comes about through increased certification required in the interests of safeguarding public health. Every abattoir has to have an official veterinary surgeon to see that it operates hygienically and that slaughtering is humane. Full-time vets are appointed to Defra's Meat Hygiene Service. Every port and airport has to have a veterinary surgeon available. No wonder vets are in short supply.

WOMEN IN THE PROFESSION

It is a fact that over three times as many women are now admitted to veterinary science courses as men (see Table 3 on page 46). They comprise about a third of all the vets in the country but they form only one in five of the sole principals in general practice. Two explanations have been suggested for this. One is that the statistic reflects past intakes into the profession and this is changing. Another is that whereas women are in the majority at age 30 or younger, they only comprise one in ten of those aged 50 or over. This suggests that they leave the profession early – perhaps in order to have a family – and do not always return. The figures also hint that they are slightly more inclined than their male colleagues to work in the public sector.

SPECIALISATION

An RCVS Manpower Survey in 2006 revealed that 72% of a vet's time is spent with small animals. In general, there is a growing trend towards specialisation within practices. Areas of specialisation include cattle, horses, household pets or even exotics. Specialisation can also be more sophisticated – for example combining equine care with lameness in all animals. Dermatology, soft tissues and cardiology are examples of the kinds of specialisation which are seen as helpful to clients. It is possible for postgraduate specialist qualifications to be obtained under the Royal College of Veterinary Surgeons' specialist certificate and diploma examinations.

TABLE 5: NUMBER AND DISTRIBUTION OF THE PROFESSION WHO ARE ECONOMICALLY ACTIVE

	2006	2005	Change
General Practice	12,975	12,506	+3.75%
Defra	421	417	+0.96%
Food Standards Agency	14	14	0.0%
Meat Hygiene Services	58	60	-3.3%
Ministry of Defence	38	39	-2.56%
NI Department of Agriculture	169	164	+2.96%
Scottish Agricultural College	58	60	-3.3%
Universities	663	732	-9.43%
Research councils	17	24	-29.17%
Industry and commerce	299	291	+2.68%
Charities	337	364	-7.42%
Other	11	14	-21.43%
Total	**15060**	**14685**	**+2.49%**

Source: Royal College of Veterinary Surgeons Annual Report 2006

DEALING WITH PEOPLE

Being in veterinary practice means that you are running a business. For example, today's vets have to be familiar with computer records on health and production and know how to interpret them, but there is a more important factor. Vets have to be customer-oriented and students soon pick this up. 'The way we approach people is crucial; it's our bread and butter,' remarked one vet. 'It's the same on the telephone. We make a point of being cheerful and reassuring with a few words of advice until we can get there.' This aspect of practice is now so important that some practices are hiring a manager to run the administrative side and help to train reception staff. Most courses now make some attempt to introduce the student to the economics of running a practice, although as one vet commented wryly, 'Few will think of bookkeeping!'

PROFESSIONAL APPROACH

With increasing professionalism and rising customer expectations go higher overheads. A student at school may not realise the significance of all the things they see in a modern surgery. Look around and first note the condition of the waiting area. It should be comfortable and clean. The kennels should be of good quality and there will probably be a separate preparation room. Notice all the new equipment, a far cry from the more primitive era described in the Herriot books. It is quite likely that there will be anaesthetic and blood pressure monitoring equipment, radiography, ultrasound and Doppler ultrasound, endoscopy units, orthopaedic instrumentation, operating microscopes and laser equipment for cataract surgery. To equip a modern veterinary surgery requires a considerable capital sum and so most newly qualified vets will start their working life by going into practice with other vets. Some will aspire to and attain a partnership after two or three moves; a few will, after gaining experience over three or four years, branch out on their own.

TEACHING AND RESEARCH A qualification in veterinary science is more than a licence to practise. It can also open up opportunities for those interested in university teaching and research at home and overseas. In addition to clinical research work, some veterinary surgeons undergo further postgraduate training in the biological sciences. Specialisation is possible in physiology, pathology, microbiology, nutrition, genetics and statistics. Veterinary scientists are not exclusively found to be working in institutions concerned with animal health and disease; they can also be found working in natural science laboratories, medical schools and medical research institutes. The opportunities are there for young veterinary surgeons attracted by a research career.

The veterinary schools provide referral hospitals to which veterinary surgeons can refer cases needing more specialised treatment. For example, recent success in the treatment of equine colic has stemmed from early recognition and referral of appropriate cases allied to developments in anaesthesia and monitoring, improved surgical techniques and suture materials plus better post-operative care. Good teamwork between the referring practitioner and the university specialists plays a big part.

Veterinary graduates are employed as research scientists by Defra, the Biotechnology and Biological Sciences Research Council, the Animal Health Trust, and in pharmaceutical and other industrial research organisations

THE GOVERNMENT

Most of the veterinary surgeons employed by Defra work in either the Meat Hygiene Service, the Veterinary Field Service or the Veterinary Investigation Service. Field officers have a wide range of responsibilities which include the control of major epidemic diseases of farm animals, matters of consumer protection largely in relation to meat hygiene, the control of import and export of animals and the operation of health schemes.

The Veterinary Investigation Service comprises officers who are based in laboratories known as veterinary investigation centres (VICs). Their job is to operate and support control schemes in the interests of public health, to monitor developments and give early warning of any disease problems or dangers to the safety of the food chain. They also provide practising vets with a chargeable diagnostic service. The Central Veterinary Laboratory

(CVL) at Weybridge employs veterinary surgeons who carry out research and support for various field activities. The Veterinary Medicines Directorate (VMD) deals with the licensing of drugs.

OTHER CAREER PATHS

Veterinary scientists are needed by the Army. Their duties arise in the Royal Army Veterinary Corps where they care for service animals, mostly working dogs and horses used for ceremonial purposes. They also have public health responsibilities and opportunities for research or post-graduate study. Those recruited join as Army captains for a four-year Short Service Commission, but this may be altered to a Regular Commission on application.

Some veterinary surgeons prefer to work for animal welfare societies, such as the RSPCA, PDSA and Blue Cross. Others work as inspectors for the Home Office.

SUMMING UP

Many students are interested in becoming veterinary surgeons. For some it will remain a pipe dream either because they lack the ability or skill, or because their ideas about being a veterinary surgeon are not rooted in reality. However, there are real opportunities for those who are motivated and determined to reach their goal. The competition is severe but not impossible and prospective students should be encouraged to explore the veterinary option early by seeking practical experience. As one vet put it, 'See a farm, get your wellies dirty, experience some blood and gore, and see that the life of a vet is not all about cuddly puppies!' This will test both resolve and suitability.

The demand for veterinary services and research-related activities is strong and is increasing. Market forces do dictate, but funding limitations on the number of places in veterinary schools imposed by the higher education funding councils are a controlling factor. Nevertheless, the profession of veterinary surgeon retains its popularity among young people. It is not because of the money, the car or accommodation, which is often next to the practice ready for instant call-outs! Nor can long hours be the attraction; the provision of a 24-hour service to the public is mandatory. Rather it is probably the sense that being a vet is a way of life rather than a job.

Is being a veterinary surgeon a unique career?

Consider for a moment that the vet has to be a general practitioner with numerous skills and specialisms. Most practitioners are self-employed with wide variations in income, depending upon the type of practice and location. Yet they must make a big capital investment in the latest equipment as veterinary medicine becomes increasingly technical. In the UK there is no state funding for veterinary practice equivalent to the NHS. All the funding comes from the clients (or charities such as the PDSA). Yet vets do not want finance to take over. It is still a caring profession that does not always charge what it should, for example for compassionate reasons. It is a profession facing immense changes and so it is not surprising that a new career is emerging, that of practice manager. A sensible appointment of a professional manager allows the vets to concentrate on what they do best: dealing with the clients and their animals.

An experienced vet, operating a mixed practice on the Wirral, put the unique qualities of being a vet this way: 'I think people respect what we do. Every Friday a lady brings us a chocolate cake. It's little things like this that make you feel appreciated.' A vet is many things – skilled surgeon, business manager, counsellor and confidant. Vets know that for their clients the animals are often the most important thing in their lives. They have tremendous responsibility for the animals, whether in sickness or in health, and when all other options have failed they have the authority and power vested in them by law to take the animal's life. They devote their lives to animal welfare but it is not based on sentimentality. Find out whether it is the life for you and if it is, go for it.

CASE STUDY   'Did my training prepare me for the realities of being a veterinary surgeon?' This is a question that Jenny, who qualified from Liverpool eight years ago, is often asked by veterinary students when they undertake work experience in her practice. Jenny's response is usually yes and no. 'The training that I got from Liverpool was excellent – I think that the balance between scientific and medical aspects of the course was just right, and the emphasis on the practical side of the profession was invaluable. The course was hard work but we felt that we were a team and that we needed to support each other and this helped enormously. When I graduated I felt confident that I could handle any of the situations I was likely to face. What I didn't expect was the need to continually learn new things. I had, unrealistically I suppose, expected that once I had trained, that would be it. I could then practise as a veterinary surgeon for the rest of my career, confident that my training had prepared me fully for the job.

'In fact, the job changes very rapidly. New treatments, new drugs, new guidelines, new laws; all of these mean that it is vital to try to keep up to date. This is sometimes hard. At the end of a long day, possibly having got very little sleep the night before because of an emergency on a local farm, the last thing I want to do is to read a long report on the effectiveness of a new treatment. However, Continuing Professional Development (CPD) is not only important for veterinary surgeons if they are to perform effectively; it is also one of the requirements of the RCVS. CPD is made easier because there are many courses and training sessions available to vets, and these also give us the opportunity to meet up with other vets in similar situations and to discuss current trends in veterinary medicine.'

Jenny has never regretted her decision to become a vet. Her interest started when she was about 16 years old when her older cousin trained as a veterinary nurse. Many of the students that Jenny studied with had made the decision to study veterinary medicine at a much earlier age, and had managed to accrue many years of relevant work experience before they applied through UCAS, whereas Jenny had a year between making the decision and her application. This meant that she had to take whatever opportunities she could to gain contact with the veterinary profession. Alongside some work-shadowing with a local vet, Jenny got a weekend job in a local pet shop which specialised in exotic animals and this brought her into contact with a wide variety of veterinary surgeons. Jenny is now working in a mixed practice near Birmingham, and hopes to become a partner in a practice in the future.

8

FURTHER INFORMATION

BRISTOL
The Veterinary Admissions Office
University of Bristol
Senate House
Tyndall Avenue
Bristol BS8 1TH
Tel: 0117 928 7679
Fax: 0117 925 1424
admissions@bris.ac.uk
www.bris.ac.uk
Contact: Katie Whatley (katie.whatley@bris.ac.uk)

CAMBRIDGE
Veterinary Admission Enquiries Adviser
Department of Veterinary Medicine
University of Cambridge
Madingley Road
Cambridge CB3 0ES
Tel: 01223 330811
Fax: 01223 337610
application.advice@vet.cam.ac.uk
www.vet.cam.ac.uk
Contact: Janet Smith (js247@cam.ac.uk)

EDINBURGH
The Admissions Officer
School of Veterinary Medicine
Royal (Dick) School of Veterinary Studies
University of Edinburgh
Easter Bush Veterinary Centre
Roslin
Midlothian
EH25 9RG
Tel: 0131 650 6138
Fax: 0131 650 6585
dickvet@ed.ac.uk
www.vet.ed.ac.uk
Contact: Geraldine Giannopoulos
(geraldine.giannopoulos@ed.ac.uk)

GLASGOW
Admissions Office
Faculty of Veterinary Medicine
University of Glasgow
Bearsden Road
Glasgow G61 1QH
Tel: 0141 330 5705
Fax: 0141 942 7215
admissions@vet.gla.ac.uk
www.gla.ac.uk/faculties/vet
Contact: Joyce Wason (j.wason@vet.gla.ac.uk)

LIVERPOOL
Admissions Sub-Dean
Faculty of Veterinary Science
The University of Liverpool
Liverpool L69 7ZJ
Tel: 0151 794 4797
Fax: 0151 794 4279
vetadmit@liv.ac.uk
www.liv.ac.uk/vets

LONDON
The Registry
Royal Veterinary College
University of London

Royal College Street
London NW1 0TU
Tel: 020 7468 5148
Fax: 020 7388 2342
registry@rvc.ac.uk
www.rvc.ac.uk
Contact: Margaret Kilyon (mkilyon@rvc.ac.uk)

NOTTINGHAM
Admissions Team
School of Veterinary Medicine and Science
University of Nottingham
Sutton Bonington Campus
College Road
Sutton Bonington
Leicestershire
LE12 5RD
Tel: 0115 951 6414
Fax: 0115 951 6415
veterinary-enquiries@nottingham.ac.uk
www.nottingham.ac.uk/vet

OTHER CONTACTS AND SOURCES OF INFORMATION

USEFUL ORGANISATIONS AND WEBSITES

Blue Cross
www.bluecross.org.uk

British Equine Veterinary Association
www.beva.org.uk

British Veterinary Association
www.bva.co.uk
The national representative body for the British veterinary profession.

Department for Environment, Food and Rural Affairs (Defra)
www.defra.gov.uk

Mander Portman Woodward
www.mpw.co.uk/getintomed
For further advice and information on getting into veterinary school, please see the website that accompanies this book.

People's Dispensary for Sick Animals
www.pdsa.org.uk

Royal College of Veterinary Surgeons
Belgravia House
62–64 Horseferry Road
London SW1P 2AF
Tel: 020 7222 2001
education@rcvs.org.uk
www.rcvs.org.uk

St George's University, Grenada
Tel: 0800 169 9061
www.sgu.edu

Society of Practising Veterinary Surgeons
www.spvs.org.uk
Provides advice to veterinary surgeons.

Super Vets
www.rvc.ac.uk/supervets
Website for the BBC series about vets at the Royal Veterinary College, London Zoo and Whipsnade Wild Animal Park.

Vetsonline
www.vetsonline.com
Online database and resource.

Universities and Colleges Admissions Service
www.ucas.co.uk

COURSES

VetCam
Tel: 01223 337701
Two-day residential 'Introduction to Veterinary Science in Cambridge' course held in March.

Vetsix
www.workshop-uk.com
Two-day conference organised by the Workshop University Conferences for interested sixth-formers and held annually at Nottingham.

PUBLICATIONS: VETERINARY MEDICINE

You and Your Vet
www.bva-awf.org.uk
Popular pet care magazine published quarterly in the interests of companion animals and their owners by the British Veterinary Association: Animal Welfare Foundation (BVA: AWF), and available exclusively from most veterinary practices. It has many useful addresses and can give you a feel for what concerns pet owners and vets.

PUBLICATIONS: GENERAL

Degree Course Offers
Brian Heap, £28.99, Trotman; www.careers-portal.co.uk

Financial Support for Students
DfES; Tel: 0870 000 2288;
www.dfes.gov.uk/studentsupport

How to Complete Your UCAS Application
£11.99, Trotman; www.careers-portal.co.uk
Works through the application procedure step by step using examples, and includes information on how to avoid the most common mistakes and how to write a winning personal statement.

Student Book
Klaus Boehm and Jenny Lees-Spalding, £16.99, Trotman; www.careers-portal.co.uk

Student Loans – A Guide to Applying
Free, Student Loans Company (100 Bothwell Street, Glasgow G2 7JD); www.slc.co.uk

Students' Money Matters
Gwenda Thomas, £14.99, Trotman; www.careers-portal.co.uk

University and College Entrance: The Official Guide
www.careers-portal.co.uk
The latest edition is normally published in June and is usually available in school and public reference libraries.